7 Biblical Truths
You Won't Hear
in Church*

*But Might
Change Your Life

7 Biblical Truths
You Won't Hear
in Church*

*But Might
Change Your Life*

DAVID R. RICH

HARVEST HOUSE PUBLISHERS

EUGENE, OREGON

Cover photo © Thinkstock / Getty Images

Cover by Terry Dugan Design, Minneapolis, Minnesota

7 BIBLICAL TRUTHS YOU WON'T HEAR IN CHURCH
Copyright © 2006 by David A. Rich
Published by Harvest House Publishers
Eugene, Oregon 97402
www.harvesthousepublishers.com
Library of Congress Cataloging-in-Publication Data

Rich, David (David A.)
7 biblical truths you won't hear in church / David A. Rich.
   p. cm.
ISBN-13: 978-0-7369-1607-3 (pbk.)
ISBN-10: 0-7369-1607-5
1. Christian life—Biblical teaching. I. Title: Seven biblical truths you won't hear in church. II. Title.
BV4501.3.R48 2006
230—dc22   2005019223

Printed in the United States of America

07 08 09 10 11 12 13 / BP-MS / 10 9 8 7 6 5 4

To Glenna Salsbury,
who "shocked" me one night into searching for truth—

for her endless patience and mentorship

Acknowledgments

I'd like to personally thank my editor, Paul Gossard, who from day one shared my enthusiasm for this book and made the process so easy it hardly seemed like work.

I'd also like to thank Glenna Salsbury, to whom I dedicated this book. Without Glenna, there would be no book. She has taught me so much about these truths and how to boldly share them with others.

I also thank Randy Harling, whose gentle critique and feedback was so valuable. He's been a role model for displaying the light of Christ and a friend for many years. Randy, I am proud to call you my pastor.

Thank you as well to Steve McVey, who wrote the foreword and provided inspiration when I needed it most.

Last, but not least, I'd like to thank my family and especially my wife, Brenda. She quietly stands by me as I debate and challenge other people about the truths in this book. It's not an easy job, but she does it with eloquence.

Contents

Foreword

David Rich is a spiritual revolutionary, a facilitator of change. He is one of those people you meet who simply don't seem to possess the ability to restrain themselves from sharing the things they're passionate about. Thank God for that. David is a man on fire—in the best sense of the word. God's grace has ignited him, and in *7 Biblical Truths You Won't Hear in Church,* some of those grace sparks will jump off on you.

This is a book that will increase your pulse rate and make your heart skip a beat. Along the way it might get you riled up—and then bring you to shed tears of joy later. And don't be surprised if you find yourself thinking at times, *This guy is dead wrong!*—only to follow up with, *Could this really be true? Can grace be* that *big and wonderful?* Save yourself the agony of trying to figure out the answer. It *is* that big and wonderful. Grace is better than this book or any other book can describe.

Can a person overestimate God's grace? That is hardly a problem in the modern church. Modern Christendom sometimes peddles a strange message—it teaches you're supposed to generously give your heart to Jesus and then spend the rest of your life breaking your back for Him. This teaching is called "grace," but never has there existed a greater misnomer.

That's why David wrote this book. His heartbeat is to lay grace out on the table in its native and pure form. I challenge you to read with an open mind. There are plenty of jewels here. If you don't like one, go to the next. Don't be surprised, though, if you come back later and pick up the one you left behind. And don't take the author's word for something, but when he demonstrates that what he has written is grounded in Scripture, be willing to have your mind changed.

May you be blessed as you read *7 Biblical Truths You Won't Hear in Church*. It may well change the way you think about God, about grace, and even about yourself!

—Dr. Steve McVey
author of *Grace Walk*

Going to the Right Source

The Bible is quite capable of being shocking all on its own, especially if you're only casually familiar with what it says. I had always gone to church, and I truly believed I understood the Bible well enough to grasp the basics. I never imagined the things I didn't know and understand could change my life and transform my relationship with God. The journey began for me one evening in the summer of 1996 when I was shocked—and that shock drove me straight to the Word. Granted, I was out to prove my shocker wrong, but I went to the right source. The more I searched, though, the more I found what I wasn't looking for, but it led me to discover many truths I had never heard in church. (More on that story later, but suffice it to say, God has become bigger and more wonderful than I ever imagined.)

If you are able to read this book with the fresh mind of a child searching for the truth, then I promise you one thing; you will be *driven* to the Word. You will be compelled to know more and understand more, and you'll want to share your newfound enthusiasms. Perhaps you will be like me and start out with a lot of questions in your mind. That's okay. My goal in this book is not to convince you that I'm right and others are wrong. I don't have all the answers. I just want to help you be clear as to what you believe. I want to help you know *all* the truths, not just a bit here and a bit there.

Why? Well, the parts of the truth I was missing were the parts that really mattered—the parts that cause us to drop to our knees and thank God daily, the parts that help us find peace and comfort in our everyday struggles. Now I'm simply doing what I feel compelled to do, and that's share my enthusiasm for truths I believe were meant for all Christians.

Keep in mind, though, that it's easier to learn something brand-new than it is to relearn something you're familiar with. I've been a professional speaker for 20 years, and I can tell you from experience that I'd rather speak to a group of rookies in a given profession than a group of jaded veterans. The old saying is true—it *is* sometimes hard to teach an old dog new tricks. However, you may be ready to learn but not even know it. When the Spirit of truth knocks on your door, He can be very hard to resist. He will guide you on a journey you may not have expected and may not have thought you even wanted (see John 16:13). That's precisely what happened to me.

∞

To help prepare the way, I want to mention two points up front. First, a word here and a word there can totally change the meaning of things. For instance, I'm almost certain you've already perused the chapter titles of this book to see if you want to read it or not. (I'll go out on a limb and say I've at least piqued your curiosity or you wouldn't be reading these words. You may agree or disagree with what's in the chapter titles, but I've got your attention.) Well, the truth of chapter 6 lies predominantly in the word *trying*. Without that single word, the meaning of the statement changes entirely. Scripture is like that as well—a word here and a word there can make a great difference.

Of course, some of the truths you'll encounter here may be more shocking to you than others. Some, you may argue, you've heard before in church. But I urge you to read with an open heart. It may be that you've heard something but didn't grasp it, or that you've only heard a part of it. I want to help you discover what you may have been missing. It's all in the Word. And of course, I don't want to present anything not grounded in Scripture, so I have quoted and listed Scripture references throughout. The Bible is, was, and always will be the only source for truth.

The second point I want to mention is that these truths may take some time to digest. I didn't understand what I was reading for the longest time, but I knew I wanted to learn more. Each truth is like a puzzle piece, and until you have an understanding of the entire puzzle, the significance of each piece may not be clear. Thus, this book may leave you with some questions as well as answers. Think of it as lighting the pilot light. Lighting the pilot light doesn't bring heat, but it's the necessary first step. I pray this spark will cause you to burn for greater understanding and be willing to explore things that might sound strange to you at first.

Finally, remember that something led you to this book. Something caused you to skim through my words to see what I might have to say. Something is definitely at work in your life. Something is fanning the flames of your curiosity. Or perhaps I should say, Someone.

1 The Truth Is Out There

I think I first heard the phrase "The truth is out there" in the '70s while watching some show about UFOs and life on other planets. The show suggested there was some elaborate cover-up scheme at work to suppress the truth that UFOs really existed—a scheme that included the highest levels of our government. I was fascinated, but not to the point where I actually bought into their theories (though some of my friends are convinced to this day that "the truth is out there somewhere").

The truth is, the truth is out there, but we need not look to the sky to find it. It can be found on bookshelves, nightstands, and dressers around the world. It's the Bible. God has never tried to cover up the truth. There may be some things we won't understand this side of heaven, but the truth is all there in Scripture. The Bible was given to us to strengthen our faith and hope in the Lord. It's key among the many glorious tools God uses to draw us closer to Him. The more I read the Bible, the more fascinated I become by it. Another name for it might be "everything you've always wanted to know about everything." Every subject of significance can be found in the Bible in some form.

However, my most interesting discovery about God's Word is that it is written for both the beginner and the advanced. It seems to adapt itself to its reader. There are easy-to-grasp stories and truths for the new believer—and there are more complex parables, prophecies, and truths for the mature Christian. Some truths are so complex that even theologians can't seem agree as to their meaning. At various stages of my life I've read parts of the Bible that were completely over my head. They might as well have been in the original Hebrew and Greek. I wouldn't know what I was reading—only later would I come back to it and understand it clearly and fully. I can't explain this any better than anyone else, but I've come to realize that understanding doesn't come from exhausting study alone. It comes from God. It comes by revelation. The Pharisees knew Scripture, but they didn't know truth. Martin Luther taught seminary for years before he came to understand what he taught. The same can also be said of the apostle Paul. It wasn't until he was struck with revelation that he came to know the truth.[1]

God reveals certain things to us at certain times, and sometimes the light goes on and we understand. Other times, we must simply accept His Word at face value, even when we don't understand what we've read. The deeper implication here, and one Paul certainly understood, is that knowing Scripture doesn't necessarily guarantee knowing truth. There are lots of learned Bible scholars in the world who will dispute even the existence of

Jesus. Knowledge is not the answer. Paul wrote in 1 Corinthians that "knowledge puffs up, but love edifies. And if anyone thinks that he knows anything, he knows nothing yet as he ought to know" (8:1-2). Those are pretty strong words, but his meaning is clear. Worldly wisdom may come from knowledge, but spiritual wisdom comes only by revelation.

A Close Encounter in San Francisco

The best example of this I can think of is drawn from my personal experience. I've been a believer for as far back as I can remember. I grew up an active member of my church and cannot recall an exact moment when I first believed. Reading the Bible hasn't always been a habit in my life, but I paid attention to my pastor's sermons and had an above-average understanding of what it said...so I thought.

It was the summer of 1996. By then, I was a grown man—three kids, two cars, and one house. I had been speaking professionally for ten years and had written my first book. I knew what I knew. My ideology was set—that is, before I had dinner one night in San Francisco with a speaker colleague of mine named Glenna Salsbury. Glenna is no ordinary speaker. At that time she was already in the speaker Hall of Fame, and she holds a master's degree in theology from Fuller Seminary.

There were a handful of us at dinner that night, but the three of us at my end of the table somehow got on the subject of religion. It's said that sex, politics, and religion are the three subjects you should avoid if you want to steer clear of controversy, but that didn't deter us. I remember the conversation starting out pretty bland at first. But before we knew it, we were debating spiritual time bombs such as predestination, free will, and the permanency of salvation. The conversation was sometimes loud, occasionally thoughtful, frequently argumentative, but altogether stimulating. With a demeanor as subtle as hitting me over the head with a sledgehammer, Glenna challenged every belief I've ever had about God. She had the gall to tell me that as far as God is concerned, I was as perfect as I'll ever be! How could that be? I hadn't been a particularly big champion for God. I had never been through seminary. I hadn't won that many souls for Christ. I had never been a missionary or even a regular Sunday-school teacher. I'd even missed my share of worship services altogether. How could I be perfect in God's eyes? She must have been off her rocker. And that one was one of the milder truths she hit me with.

I left the dinner table that night and went straight to the hotel copy of the Bible in my room with the sole intent of finding passages to prove Glenna wrong. I just knew I would find enough evidence to confront her the next morning and preserve my system of beliefs. There was only one problem. I couldn't do it. The deeper I dug into the Word, the more intrigued I became. I can't say I agreed with all she said yet—that took years—but I was convicted enough to want to know more!

Beginning a Journey

That was the start of a five-year journey for truth that included weekly phone calls and e-mails to Glenna. Every time I thought I understood one point, I found a passage that seemed to contradict it. I felt like a ratchet wrench. Every time I made one click forward, I'd wind up going two clicks back. God chose to reveal His truths to me very slowly and deliberately despite my prayers to the contrary. I've never been a patient person, to say the least, and I wanted to fit all the pieces together overnight. But that's not always the way it works. Some things take time. I began to understand exactly what Paul meant when he wrote in his first letter to the church in Corinth, "I fed you with milk and not with solid food; for until now you were not able to receive it, and even now you are still not able" (1 Corinthians 3:2).

Which leads me to the present day. My writing this book doesn't mean in any way that I have all the answers. I certainly do not. I continue to learn and relearn every day as the Lord leads me. My sole aim for writing these words is to serve as a catalyst to drive people to the Bible to discover what the Lord may be trying to show them. The truths that I present in this book have completely energized my faith and strengthened my love for God. They may have the same effect on you; but even if you do not agree with my words, hopefully they will strengthen whatever you may believe. It's more important than ever to know what you believe and why you believe it. Dare to be like the Bereans "who searched the Scriptures daily" to see if what Paul was saying was true (Acts 17:11).

The Truth Presents a Challenge

We're living in an age of the religious smorgasbord. Many simply pick and choose what feels right to them, regardless of whether or not it is grounded in real truth. Some of the blame for this must fall squarely on the shoulders of the modern church, although its roots can be traced back to the time just after the resurrection. Now don't misunderstand me. There are many excellent churches across America that teach the truth and nothing but the truth. I speak in such churches all the time. There are many that are doing awesome things for the kingdom of God and are led by wonderful people. I go to such a church. My pastor is a shining example of how God uses people to lead others. He

I've witnessed too many sermons that could just have easily been given in a corporate boardroom rather than a place of worship. They were filled with tried and tested self-help recipes that I myself have been dishing out to corporate audiences for almost 20 years.

teaches straight from the Word and isn't afraid to tackle the tough issues.

But that isn't the case everywhere. Many churches I've visited and heard from very purposely shy away from truths that may ruffle a few feathers. The apostle Paul warned of the day when people would not believe the truth but rather those who would tell them what their "itching ears" want to hear (2 Timothy 4:3). I've visited many churches where people don't even bring a Bible and where the pastor preaches a sermon without referencing a single scriptural passage. I've witnessed too many sermons that could just have easily been given in a corporate boardroom rather than a place of worship. They were filled with tried and tested self-help recipes that I myself have been dishing out to corporate audiences for almost 20 years.

Part of the reason for my ministry today is because I've grown leery and weary of the entire self-help movement of which I've been a part. I have an increasingly hard time standing in front of people telling them how to be successful without telling them how they can live successfully in Christ. And too many pastors have jumped on this popular bandwagon. I've even heard one sermon based around the old notion that God helps those who help themselves. That may sound right on the surface, but it's not biblical truth.

More on that later, but too many churches have become so vanilla in their teaching that one has to look real hard to find any glimmer of truth in it. I can only wager an educated guess as to why so many teach what feels good rather than what is actually true. My guess is fear. Fear of losing a parishioner, fear of losing money, and fear of not being popular head the list. I've personally known pastors who have admitted to being afraid of tackling the tough issues for fear of the backlash that may result. Fear is natural, of course; some fear is even healthy. The writer of the letter to the Hebrews might have felt this fear when he wrote,

> *The word of God is living and powerful, and sharper than any two-edged sword, piercing even to the division of soul and spirit, and of joints and marrow, and is the discerner of the thoughts and intents of the heart* (4:12).

The truth can be sharp, and many churches have sacrificed truth for the appearance of peace and harmony. This flies in the face, however, of what Jesus warned us of in Matthew 10:34, "Do not think that I came to bring peace on earth. I did not come to bring peace but a sword." The truth is out there, and it can hurt when it exposes something we've kept hidden.

Two Perspectives on Truth—and They're Both True

Many try to avoid the challenge of the truth in another way. From the results of a 2001 Barna Research survey,[2] it's reasonable to conclude that about 78 percent of adult Americans don't believe in absolute truth (nor are they sure what they do believe, it seems). Therefore the Bible cannot contain such truth.

I even once had a debate with a gentleman who cited the Bible itself as a case for no absolute truth. His argument was that the Bible was contradictory and therefore could not contain absolute truth. Such arguments make me shake my head in disbelief, but it's a common misconception. Many people do believe the Bible contradicts itself, so how could it be true?

There are countless passages that, if held up side by side, do indeed appear to be saying completely opposite things. For example, 1 John 4:8 says that "God is love," yet it says in Isaiah 45:7 that God "creates calamity," and in Malachi 1:3 and Romans 9:13 that God hated Esau. It doesn't make any sense. That is the only logical conclusion you can come to when you take passages out of context and hold them up side by side. You'll never find a full understanding of the truth by looking at individual passages. That will only bring frustration and lead to misinterpretation.

However, when you study the Bible in total, you will find that nowhere does it contradict itself. We may not understand it all, but that doesn't make it contradictory. Shortly after the verse in Isaiah that tells us God "creates calamity," Isaiah 55:8 warns us, "'My thoughts are not your thoughts, nor are your ways My ways' says the Lord. 'For as the heavens are higher than the earth, so are My ways higher than your ways, and My thoughts than your thoughts.'" Right after Romans 9:13, in which God says He hated Esau, is Romans 9:21: "Does not the potter have power over the clay, from the same lump to make one vessel for honor and another for dishonor?" I don't necessarily understand this any better than you might, but I get what God is saying. He's saying He is God and we're not. Period. He doesn't have to make sense to us. Both passages are biblically accurate and completely noncontradictory. From our perspective, He's the potter and we're the clay. And from His perspective, it's all out of love.

This gets us to the heart of the matter. Fueling the debate over biblical contradiction is the fact that the Bible does teach truths from two perspectives. There's our very limited human perspective, and there's God's infinite perspective. It's not a matter of one being right and one being wrong. Both are right, but obviously God's perspective is the one that matters. Here's an illustration: When reporters interviewed soldiers who landed on the shores of Normandy in World War II, they found they all pretty much thought the same thing—that they were doomed. They were doing their duty but didn't have an overwhelming sense of optimism, to say the least. However, when interviewing those who flew overhead in air missions, the reporters discovered they said almost the opposite. They knew right away the mission would be a success. The only difference between those on the ground, who thought the mission was doomed, and the ones in the air, who knew it would be successful, was perspective. We're like the ground troops. We can only see the things in our limited line of sight. God sees everything. The Bible teaches truths from both perspectives.

Who's Holding onto Whom?

Another way to look at this is shown by an analogy I ran across a few years ago, I believe in one of R.C. Sproul's wonderful books. I've since come to call it "the analogy of grips." It's one that everyone who has ever taken a child grocery-shopping can relate to. When a person is escorting a child across a crowded parking lot by the hand, there are two grips at work. The first is the child's rather questionable grip on the guardian. If your children were like my children, their grip was undependable at best. Sometimes they would grip firmly, while other times they did everything in their power to break free.

The strength of their grip would come and go with mood swings, but it didn't matter—because there was a second grip also at work. That was the guardian's—my—grip on the child.

Thank God, for the child's safety was not based on the child's grip, but on the guardian's grip. Recalling my own experience, there were times I clung to my child's hand by just their pinky finger. My knuckles were white with effort, but they weren't going anywhere. I saw to that. Sure, from their perspective they were imprisoned slaves—but from my perspective, they were safe in my care. There were two grips—albeit one was sometimes rather questionable—and two different perspectives for the same occurrence.

The same is true of the Bible. It teaches truths from both perspectives. There's no doubt it does contain passages that teach us as God's children how to have a tighter grip on the Father. But there are also truths that teach us we are firmly safe in the Father's hand. He's got us no matter how hard we sometimes try to get away. Sure, we feel closer to God when we're gripping back, but that's only a human feeling. Parents don't love their children less when they're misbehaving. The child may be punished, but parents love their children no matter what. Ideally, parents try to teach their kids how to behave, not to earn favor and love, but to learn how to reciprocate love and be responsible people.

I refer to the parts of the Bible that teach us how to grip back as "child's grip" passages. St. Augustine called them exhortations. They are practical and tactical. Conversely, I call the parts that teach us to find peace and rest in God's guardianship "Father's grip" passages. It's important to know and recognize which passages are which. Otherwise, we can become obsessed with gripping when we should be resting and vice versa. Both are important.

In too many churches, however, gripping is all that's talked about. In fact, too much emphasis on gripping the Father's hand can promote trying to please God with good works. And that's not what the passages were meant to promote. The child's grip passages are there to help us *feel* closer to God—not to actually *make* us closer to God. Believers are already as close to God as they'll ever be. (More on that later on.)

An unbalanced preoccupation with child's-grip passages can keep Christians from finding peace and rest. I've known many believers who are obsessed with gripping. They want to grip firmly all the time, and they beat themselves up when they can't do it. They always wonder whether they're gripping hard enough and whether they should be using the other hand. One woman even told me she feared if she didn't always keep a tight hold, God might let go. She told me that her pastor once told her that could happen if she stopped coming to and giving to the church. Nothing could be further from the truth, but she remained nervous and fearful despite my attempts to reassure her with the truth—that God wasn't about to let go.

∽

A theologian once lamented to me that most people don't want to know the truth, but only what sounds and feels right. He further commented that controversy was not good for the church. The image that comes to mind is that of Jack Nicholson on the stand in *A Few Good Men,* saying, "You can't handle the truth." I beg to differ. We not only can handle it; we want it. The problem is, it's been all too hard to find.

That's precisely why I am compelled to write this book. There are plenty of books to read and places to go that will further the cause of common beliefs and popular religion. But people are craving the plain, unadorned truth. The truths I write about are some of the more challenging ones the Bible has to offer, and some people have simply chosen to stay away from them. My goal, though, is not to convince you, or even convict you of truth. That only comes by revelation. But I do hope to inspire you to go to the Word, just as I was inspired that night in San Francisco. The Bible is and always has been our only source for truth. The truth is indeed out there. And who knows—it just might set you free.[3]

Part One
The Seven Truths

2

God Doesn't Grade on a Curve

While driving the other day through the state of North Carolina, I saw one of those huge billboards on the side of the highway that advertise a "message from God." I'm sure you've seen them. This one really caught my attention. It read, *Don't Make Me Come Down There,* and it was signed, *God.* I almost swallowed the gum I was chewing. While I can always appreciate a reminder to stay focused on God, the message is clearly more humorous than truthful. In fact, theologically speaking, it's quite absurd. First of all, God is already down here. He's present in everything, everywhere. The sign implies that God is perched on some heavenly lookout tower poised to swoop down and wreak havoc on all who get too far out of line. Which brings me to the second reason for the sign's absurdity. It also implies there are some things God overlooks and some things He just cannot ignore. It reminds me of the countless times I threatened my children, "Don't make me get up out of this chair!"

Degrees, Comparisons, and Categories

Somewhere along the way, we've adopted the notion that God views some sins as greater than others. If I stop and think about it, I understand how we can come to this conclusion. I reinforce this notion all the time with my own children. Just the other day, my older son took my younger son on a joyride on his scooter while his mother and I were out for the afternoon. We had expressly forbidden him from riding the scooter when we weren't home. This was a house rule. It was well known. He did it anyway.

Upon our return, my wife smelled gasoline where the scooter was kept and feared the boys had taken it for a joyride. Trustingly, I told her it was probably just the combination of paint, oil, and gasoline stockpiled in our crowded garage, but I offered to feel the scooter's engine to see if it was hot. Sure enough, it was. So we confronted the boys. My older son rightly confessed immediately, but my younger son held fast to his story that he had nothing to do with the ill-fated adventure. I assured him that lying was far worse than the original offense. Only upon learning that his older brother had let the cat out of the bag did he relent. He pleaded for mercy and begged for the lesser punishment that came with telling the truth. I'm sorry to report, he got it.

Mom and dads grade on a curve. It happens all the time. We're subjective creatures. In fact, our entire judicial system grades on a curve. Some offenses are worse than others. I'm not sure such a list officially exists, but society ranks offenses from most horrific to barely blinking twice. I doubt that anyone reading this would argue that capital murder is worse than a little white lie, or that breaking and entering is worse than taking a pen home from work. Those are relatively easy to discern, but society also grades the severity of similar crimes.

We've even got degrees. First-degree murder is worse than second- or third-degree murder. One can then also be charged with one count, two counts, and so on of any offense. It reminds me of poker—murder beats manslaughter, manslaughter beats assault, assault beats harassment. Each have sliding scales of severity, and because of that, judges have discretion over how severe punishments should be—and that's only after a jury of people has found us guilty in the first place. Even after someone's been found guilty, one can still earn leniency with good behavior in prison.

It's All the Same to Him—and It's All Important

Ranking, categorizing, and grading evil acts on a curve is a necessary part of a civil society. Human law is colored with shades of gray, but it's all black-and-white with God. He distinguishes between human law and His law. Paul warned us of this in Colossians 2:8 when he wrote,

Beware lest anyone cheat you through philosophy and empty deceit, according to the tradition of men, according to the basic principles of the world, and not according to Christ.

While Paul may not be exclusively speaking of laws, he does make it clear that God does not adhere to the basic principles of the world. God's got a higher standard, and He's a tough cookie.

With God, it's all or nothing. No jury, no pleading for leniency, no throwing yourself on the mercy of the court. It's one strike, you're out. The words of James 2:10 are all too clear: "Whoever shall keep the whole law, and yet stumble in one point, he is guilty of all." God doesn't grade on a curve. Either you're a sinner or you're not. If you've ever broken even the smallest of His laws, you're a sinner. As hard as it may be to fathom, murder and a little white lie are one and the same to Him. They are both against His law.

Who's to say what is trivial and what is not? Human law may recognize trivial offenses, but not God. Everything is trivial, and everything is critical.

I once ran across a young woman who vehemently declared that God is concerned with the big picture. She went on to explain that He doesn't get too involved with the minute details of our lives, and consequently doesn't pay too much attention to trivial offenses. I wanted to argue that God is in the details—all details. If God counts and numbers hairs on my head (Matthew 10:30), He is certainly a detail kind of guy. Second, no one can escape God's gaze. He sees everything, large and small. Hebrews 4:13 states, "There is no creature hidden from His sight, but all things are naked and open to the eyes of Him to whom we must give account." I don't know about you, but standing naked before God at all times is an intimidating thought. Lastly, who's to say what is trivial and what is not? Human law may recognize trivial offenses, but not God. Everything is trivial, and everything is critical.

Not Just Actions, But Thoughts As Well

As tough a pill as that may be to swallow, it gets even tougher. In addition to God's not grading our *actions* on a curve, He doesn't grade our *thoughts* on a curve either. Bad thoughts are just as bad as bad actions. Jesus taught us this in Matthew 5. In verse 20 He sets up this truth by saying,

I say to you, that unless your righteousness exceeds the righteousness of the scribes and Pharisees, you will by no means enter the kingdom of Heaven.

Wow—what a statement! The scribes and the Pharisees were considered to be shoo-ins for heaven. They were known for being zealous for keeping the law.

But that's exactly the point Jesus is trying to make. Keeping the law is more than good deeds. The law must be kept in action, in thought, and in word. It must be kept as a whole, or it's not kept at all. He went on to teach that murder was more than an action. Murder is an obvious sin, but He said in verse 22 that "whoever is angry with his brother" is guilty of murder. In verses 27-28, He continues,

You have heard that it was said to those of old, "You shall not commit adultery." But I say to you that whoever looks at a woman to lust for her has already committed adultery with her in his heart.

Well, I can't speak for you, but I get angry with someone or admire the opposite sex in some form just about every day of my life.

Jesus was trying to teach His hearers that to live by the law means it's all or nothing. Very few people commit physical murder, but everyone gets angry. (He added in verses 38-39 that even if another person harms *us*, we should not retaliate but turn the other cheek.) Very few people commit physical adultery, but everyone notices an attractive person.

God doesn't grade on a curve. We're all guilty of breaking the law. There was only one person who walked the face of the

Earth who was able to keep the entire law, and that was Jesus. We are not only reconciled to God by Christ's death but we are "saved by His life" (Romans 5:10). Thankfully, Christ fulfilled the requirements of the law for us. But make no mistake, we aren't going to do it if left to ourselves.

The Pharisees and the teachers of the law falsely believed that power was in the law. They thought all they had to do was do good. But that isn't enough. This is best illustrated by the story of the rich young ruler in the Gospels.[4] A rich young man came running up to Jesus and asked Him what he had to "do" to get into heaven. "Why do you call Me good?" Jesus replied. "No one is good but One, that is, God." Jesus was teaching and testing. He was teaching him that no one is able to keep the law, and was testing the young man to see if he knew who He was.

The young man explained he had been a good boy and had kept all of God's commandments. Certainly Jesus knew this was foolish, but He didn't scold the young man. He could have said, "Oh, yeah—you think you've been so good, but you're wrong." Instead He said, "Okay, if you want to be perfect, go, sell what you have and give it to the poor, and you will have treasure in heaven; and come, follow Me."

But the young man got sad and walked away because he was very wealthy and didn't want to part with his stuff. Jesus was unwilling to grade on a curve. The young man had led a pretty good life, but good is not good enough. The old saying goes, "Pretty good is only for horseshoes and hand grenades." Pretty good is not good enough for God. God requires perfection, and Jesus set the standard: "You shall be perfect, just as your Father in heaven is perfect" (Matthew 5:48).

Don't We Get a Break Somewhere?

And to make matters worse (actually, it only *seems* bad—it's really *good* news), God not only judges thoughts and actions, He judges *non*-thoughts, *non*-actions, and motives. We not only sin by what we say or do, we sin by what we don't say or don't do, and by the reasons behind our sins as well. James, the brother of Jesus, writes, "To him who knows to do good and does not do it, to him it is sin."[5]

This reminds me of the old story about a woman who had a dream one night that Jesus was going to stop by her house the next day. Upon waking, she started busily tidying things up. If Jesus was to stop by, she wanted Him to see a clean house. She was interrupted in her business three times. Once by a young girl selling cookies, another time by a neighbor she didn't know, who wanted to borrow something, and a final time by an old man looking for a handout. Each time she quickly sent them away. The Lord was stopping by, and she couldn't spare the time. She stayed up late that night waiting, looking out the window every time she heard a noise. But no Jesus. She finally went to bed disappointed and asked God what happened. "Why didn't Jesus stop by like He said He would?" God replied, "He did. He tried three times. The first time as a young girl, the next time as a neighbor, and the final time as an old man." You might have heard that story a bit differently, but you get the drift. Failing to do "good" when we should is sin.

Part of this problem is that we often don't recognize good when we see it. In Luke 10:38-42, Luke tells of the time Jesus went to the home of a woman named Martha. Martha's sister, Mary, immediately sat down at Jesus' feet and listened to Him. Martha was busy getting things ready, just like the woman in the old tale.

She grew angry because she was doing all the work, and she asked Jesus to tell her sister to help. He replied in verses 41-42,

> *Martha, Martha, you are worried and troubled about many things. But one thing is needed, and Mary has chosen that good part, which will not be taken away from her.*

Mary recognized that what was needed was to just rest at Jesus' feet. Martha may have been doing "good" to the rest of the world, but in Jesus' eyes, she was toiling in vain.

As for motive, God doesn't give us a break there either. If it were possible to be perfect in everything we did, and we somehow managed miraculously to do, think, and say all the right things at the right time, but didn't do them for the right reasons, we'd still be as guilty as we could be. Sin is not just an action or a thought; it's also a motive. Churches, sadly, are often filled with people who are there for the wrong reasons. Some go to feel worthier of God; others go as their weekly good deed. Spouses may go to please their mates; parents may go because it's good for the kids. Kids may go because they are forced, and some go out of sheer guilt. For some, it is just good business to show up at the right church.

But God knows the motives of the heart. Scripture is full of places that warn us about having the proper motive. For instance, 2 Corinthians 9:7 states we should give for the right reasons, not grudgingly or out of necessity. Jesus Himself tells us in Matthew 6:1-4 that any charitable things we do should be done in private, and not to seek recognition or a reward. God knows and sees all you do, think, say; don't do, don't think, don't say; and all your motives to boot. Nothing escapes His eyes—and He demands nothing short of perfection at all times!

You'd Better Give Up

Now, if my calculations are correct, right about now you are probably screaming "Stop, stop! I get it. Enough already—we have to be perfect because God doesn't cut us any slack." To which I say, "You're right—but there is a silver lining." The good news (which is what *gospel* means in Greek), is that, as believers, we *are* perfect in Christ. I'll explain that in greater detail later, but for now, it's important to understand that with God, it is all or nothing. There is only alive or dead, right or wrong, saved or not saved—there are no in-betweens.

This is an important truth to understand because, humanly, we want to pick and choose our goodness. We say to ourselves, *It's okay to take a few office supplies from work because I ran an errand for my boss on my own time.* Picking, choosing, and deciding which sins are trivial and which are the biggies is a completely human tendency, and one that isn't biblical at all. I once met a young man who explained it like this. He told me that it's kind of like "a heavenly bank account." As long as he makes "more deposits than withdrawals," he's in good shape. I told him the reality was, the very first time he made a withdrawal the account was emptied and closed forever. He thought that was a bit harsh, but I explained to him that I didn't make the rules. God did, and the reason I shared this truth with him wasn't to depress him, but to make him more aware and appreciative of God's mercy.

If you're a believer, your account has been closed, and a new account has been opened in Christ's name. You're a very wealthy person, but you can't make another deposit or withdrawal. As Christians we just get the benefits of this new account. We simply live off the interest—or, to put it another way, we live off the blessings granted us by the blood of Jesus. It's a truth that makes you want to look upward and yell, "Hallelujah!"

Let me ask a very interesting question. I'd like you to ponder it for a moment. We've spent the entire chapter thus far exploring the truth that God doesn't grade on a curve. But does He grade (and judge) believers and unbelievers differently? Think about it. Our natural first answer is, "Of course—believers get a free pardon." But that would be wrong. The answer is a resounding *no*. God is just and fair and judges everyone the same way. He measures every person against His perfect law.

Let me explain. Believers are saved by grace, a free gift from God. The Holy Spirit enters us, and we become one with Jesus. We know this from 1 Corinthians 6:17 and also Ephesians 2:18, among others. In the book of Hebrews, it proclaims that God doesn't even remember our lawless deeds anymore.[6] The unbeliever, on the other hand, is being judged on his or her own performance. God doesn't remember the sins of believers because He sees perfection in the image of Jesus. Here's a great mind-teaser question to ponder: true or false—only perfect people get to heaven. Well, what is your answer? The answer is, *true*. Heaven is a perfect place, and if we want to get there, we need to also be perfect. I'll deal with the issue of identity later, but suffice it to say for right now that if we believe in Jesus, we are perfect in Him.

Believing in Jesus is quite literally our saving grace. Anything else falls devastatingly short. This truth is summed up best by Paul in his letter to the Romans: "Whatever is not from faith is sin" (14:23). That means unbelief itself is a sin. In fact, it's the only unforgivable sin. It's unforgivable because without Jesus, we have no hope of fulfilling God's requirements. If it were somehow miraculously possible for you to lead a perfectly sinless life (which, hopefully, I've shown can't be done), but you didn't believe in Jesus, it would all be for naught. Unbelief is sin.

So, let's sum up. God gave us His requirements and His standard is perfection, not only in deed, but in thought as well. He knows what He wants, and He expects no less. He is the same yesterday, today, and tomorrow. He is just and completely fair. All our attempts at goodness on our own or qualifying for heaven on our own are as useless as "filthy rags."[7] Heaven is only for perfect people!

Thank God, through faith in Jesus, His perfection is credited to us! All that is required is full and complete surrender. I'm reminded of a story I've heard many times through the years. A man dies and is met at the gates of heaven by St. Peter, who tells the man to recap his life. He needs 1000 merit points to enter heaven. The man starts making a list: "I was raised in a church. My father was a pastor, and I held many official duties throughout the church. I went to a Christian school and on to a Bible college and was active in my church. I gave 30 percent of my income faithfully to the church each week and went on countless mission trips. I taught Sunday school for years and regularly attended Sunday-morning, Sunday-evening, and Wednesday-evening services. I never had a drink, I never lied, and I never cheated on my wife of over 40 years. We have three children, all of whom are studying to become preachers themselves. I was a bank president, and I supported my community by giving to the poor, working with the local prison ministry, and offering low-interest loans to the people who were the most needy."

The man pauses. "How am I doing so far?" Peter answers, "Well, that's about one-and-a-half points." The man cries out, "Good Lord, have mercy!" Peter smiles and says, "Now you've got it. Come on in."

God wants us to throw ourselves on His mercy. He simply asks that we agree with His declaration that we are sinners, and He invites us to believe on Him as the only righteous One. Then, and only then, will we truly begin to understand and appreciate the work of the cross. Then, and only then, will we begin to understand grace. Then, and only then, will we not fear the truth that God doesn't grade on a curve!

3

Dead People Can't Help Themselves

Order matters. The age-old debate over which came first, the chicken or the egg, is a ridiculous one to me. Of course the chicken came before the egg. The Creator always comes before the creation. End of debate. It's simply a matter of order.

Okay, I know some may take exception to my unwillingness to engage in the debate further, but I have a very reliable source on the matter. It's called the Bible. Genesis 1 tells us that God created every living creature. Just as He created man, He also created fish, trees, sheep, birds, and chickens. Therefore, the question over which came first is really nothing more than a question on whether or not you believe the Bible. Creationists will always say, the chicken. Only evolutionists might argue, the egg. It's not an insignificant debate. If you believe in the inerrancy of Scripture, the chicken-and-the-egg question is a matter of fact. Only if you do not believe the Bible is fact can you argue it any other way. Order matters. Which came first is significant to God.

You First—or God First?

The order question I want to address in this chapter is not about chickens and eggs. It's about life itself. It's the question about how believers become saved. Do you believe, and then as a result of your belief become born again—or do you become born again and then begin to believe? Think about it. It's not doublespeak. The order of events is highly important, and it's my contention that a lot of today's churches get it wrong.

Many Christians would say that you believe first, then get saved. I've sat in my share of congregations listening to the preacher talk about the importance of the decision to accept Christ. Sermons declaring the need to pray the "Sinner's Prayer" are plentiful. The prayer goes something like this: "God, I acknowledge I am a sinner, and I ask Jesus to come into my heart. He died for me, and I accept him today as my Lord and Savior." The Sinner's Prayer is based on the idea that you have come to believe in Jesus and now want to formally ask Him for salvation.

In support of this, preachers often quote what is undoubtedly the most famous passage in the Bible, John 3:16: "God so loved the world that He gave His only begotten Son, that whoever believes in Him should not perish but have everlasting life." This passage, if seen and read alone, would lead us to conclude that we need to believe *first,* then we'll be saved. But that's not biblically correct. The words are right, the premise is right, the order is wrong. Whoever does believe will indeed have eternal life, but John 3:3 has been left out. We'd never believe if we weren't first born again, as Jesus told Nicodemus. In 1 John 4:19, John writes, "We love Him because He first loved us." The apostle didn't *have* to make a point of what came first. He could have just said that we love God and He loves us. But the order makes a difference.

You Can't See It...

To best understand this truth, let's start at the beginning. What exactly happened in the Garden of Eden? You remember the story. Adam and Eve were enjoying the most heavenly (literally) life until Satan tempted Eve and they ate the forbidden fruit. It was then that sin entered the world—but it's what happened as a result of that first sin that is crucial to understand. God warned Adam and Eve what would happen. He made it quite plain: "In the day that you eat of it you shall surely die" (Genesis 2:17). Not die eventually when you get old and gray, but die the very same day. God was not speaking about physical death. He was speaking of spiritual death. Adam and Eve didn't drop dead physically at the moment they ate the fruit. In fact, they went on to live long lives and have children, but they did die spiritually. They died spiritually at the exact moment God warned they would.

So you might be asking, "What is spiritual death?" Well, I'm glad you asked. Spiritual death is hard to discern. It can't be recognized with the human eye. We interact with people every day who are spiritually dead. They look like everyone else. In many cases, they act like everyone else, but they are dead spiritually. The condition isn't noticeably painful; it's worse than physical death, though. Spiritual death means separation from God. Isaiah 59:2 tells us that in so many words: "Your iniquities have separated you from your God." The prophet Isaiah goes on to explain what that means. God is still out there, but you can't have Him. It's like you're living in another world and the line of communication to God has been cut off. His face is hidden from us and He will not hear us. He is off limits. That's spiritual death—to be cut off from Him.

Now don't get the wrong picture. Don't picture a merciless God who would have us cry out to Him but refuse to hear us. That reminds me of when my kids were young—they'd throw a temper tantrum, cover their ears, and yell, "I'm not listening!" That's not the picture at all. If we're spiritually dead, we don't *want* to cry out to God. If we did, He would listen—but people who are spiritually dead don't want to have anything to do with God.

The best description of this is found in Paul's letter to the Romans. In chapter 3 he writes, "There is none righteous, no, not one; there is none who understands; there is none who seeks after God" (verse 10). He is talking about those who are spiritually dead. They may acknowledge a generic God or cosmic force, but the God of the Bible is out of the question. I personally know a guy who can make the most articulate, brilliant presentation as to why the God of the Bible is nothing more than analogy and myth. He describes God in impersonal terms such as energy and cosmic life force. I've tried to debate him on numerous occasions, but it's all in vain. He's spiritually dead.

He's not alone. In fact, there are many in our world today who claim to believe in God and even go as far as to pray—but if they do not know Jesus, they are not praying to the true God. God does not hear the prayers of those who are not spiritually alive, and you can't be alive without Jesus. Again, we must talk about order.

...But It's Still the Case

This reminds me of the old story sometimes used to talk about salvation. Because of sin, it's said, we are floating down the river of despair, and until we accept the lifeline God has thrown us (Jesus Christ), we won't be saved. We must first grab the line to be successfully pulled to safety. And unfortunately, many people choose not to grab the line. It's a variation of the popular belief that God helps those who help themselves.

Well, I've got problems with that notion. The order is wrong. It implies that God's help is secondary—it depends

> **What happens when you throw a dead person a life preserver? Nothing. They can't choose to grab it, and no amount of coaching and yelling from the banks of the river will help. They can't hear you. They are dead.**

on our helping ourselves first. That's not biblical. As for our condition, well, we're not casually floating down the river—we're being swept away! We're dead. What happens when you throw a dead person a life preserver? Nothing. They can't choose to grab it, and no amount of coaching and yelling from the banks of the river will help. They can't hear you. They are dead. This is the condition we are born into, thanks to Adam and Eve. In 1 Corinthians 15:22, Paul tells us that "in Adam all die." Again, he is not speaking about physical death, but rather spiritual death. We are dead to God because of sin. We can't grab the life preserver, and we don't seek after God. It's simply impossible.

So you might ask, "How does one get saved?" The easy answer, of course, is that we must be born again. The reason we *must* be born again is because we are born dead. I know that sounds weird, but it's true. When we're born, we're alive physically but dead spiritually. Jesus explains this in the Gospel of John.[8] Unless we are born again, we won't be saved: "That which is born of the flesh is flesh, and that which is born of the Spirit is spirit," He explains. We have to be born again because just being born physically is insufficient. Being born physically gives us temporary human life, but only Jesus gives us eternal life.

We must become alive spiritually before we can enter heaven. We are dead until the Lord awakens us first. It's all a matter of order.

When a Dead Man Comes Alive...

Many might argue that being awakened spiritually is as easy as asking Jesus into our hearts. That brings us right back to the "Sinner's Prayer," which we talked about earlier in this chapter. It may seem like a minor point of distinction, but it's a big truth. A dead person can't, won't, or wouldn't want to ask Jesus into their heart. A dead person is dead to Jesus. Jesus does the work first. Order matters. Jesus regenerates our hearts so that we want to ask Him into our lives. He replaces our heart of stone with a heart that wants to know Him. Ezekiel 36:26-27 says exactly what I'm talking about:

> I will give you a new heart and put a new spirit within you; I will take the heart of stone out of your flesh and give you a heart of flesh. I will put My Spirit within you and cause you to walk in My statutes, and you will keep My judgments and do them.

Jesus does the work first. We respond, but He initiates.

Another example that shows the importance of order is the story of Lazurus. You might remember that one. Lazarus of Bethany dies, and Jesus brings him back to life. It's written about in John 11. Let's examine it more closely so we can see the glory of the truth.

Lazarus was sick, very sick. Jesus knew him well. In fact, you could call them friends. Lazarus was the brother of Martha and Mary. (Mary was the one who had anointed Jesus' feet with oil and wiped them with her hair.) Martha and Mary sent word to

Jesus to inform Him of Lazarus's decline and to ask Him to help. When He was told, however, Jesus' response was rather peculiar. He told the messengers that Lazarus's sickness was not "unto death," meaning he would not die. The sisters must have been puzzled. Why was Jesus not more concerned? Then to top it off, Jesus delayed two more days before going to see him. What must Martha and Mary been thinking? Here is their brother, deathly ill, and Jesus takes His good ol' time before going to him. They might have thought Jesus had flipped His lid. They might have even been mad at Him.

Have you ever been mad at God because He didn't respond the way you thought He should? It's okay—I know I have. Anyway, back to the story. On His way to see Lazarus, Jesus informs His followers that Lazarus is sleeping but He intends to wake him up. His disciples again think He's crazy, and they reply, "Lord, if he sleeps he will get well." Jesus then tells them plainly that Lazarus is dead. Jesus used the temporary word *sleep* because He was going to wake him up just as one would wake someone from a nap.

Then Jesus said another thing that must have truly puzzled those around: "I am glad for your sakes that I was not there, that you might believe. Nevertheless let us go to him." What? How insensitive! Not only did Jesus linger while Lazarus died, but now He says He was glad He wasn't there. I can only imagine the look on the faces of those around.

By the time Jesus finally did get to Lazarus, he had been dead for four days and was already in his tomb. It was a bit late for miracles, some might have thought. Martha, his sister, was among the first to greet Jesus. She began by saying what many were thinking— "Lord, if You had been here, my brother would not have died." Jesus calmly replied, "I am the resurrection and the life. He who believes in Me, though he may die, he shall live." Again, this may sound like doublespeak, but Jesus is distinguishing the difference between dying physically and living spiritually. By now, Mary had also joined them. Everyone wept for Lazarus, including Jesus. Jesus then made His point. He cried out, "Lazarus, come forth!" As you might expect, Lazarus himself walked out of his own tomb, healthy and alive as could be.

...There Are Some Lessons to Be Learned

There are so many truths to be learned from this event. First is the difference between physical and spiritual life and death. Jesus lingered because it didn't matter. Physical death is inevitable for all of us. Our bodies get old, sometimes sick, get gray and wrinkled, and then die. Lazarus died physically, but that wasn't the end of Lazarus. Jesus imparts life everlasting. Jesus is the key to eternal, spiritual life. If physical and spiritual death were the same thing, Jesus might have been in more of a hurry to get to His friend. Life everlasting is spiritual. Physical life is not.

The second truth is that Jesus calls first, and we simply respond. Lazarus is the perfect example of all of us. We're all spiritually dead before Jesus comes calling. Lazarus was even physically dead. His body was already in rapid decay. He was already in his tomb. But he still responded. He walked right out of his tomb when commanded. Something had to happen to Lazarus before he could respond to the Lord's voice. He had to be made alive by the Spirit. He had to be chosen by God. Same with us. When Jesus chooses to replace our heart of stone with one to know Him, we respond. Jesus Himself tells us in John 15:16, "You did not choose Me, but I chose you." There's no debating or decision to be made. God acted, we reacted. Order matters.

A third truth in the story could also be that, when Jesus calls, we *will* respond. The truth is, Lazarus could not have decided to stay dead. He was chosen to become alive, and that's exactly what he did. When Jesus calls, response is automatic. He calls, we answer. We cannot resist His call. Jesus tells us in John 6:37 that "all that the Father gives Me will come to Me." It's not a matter of *if*. We will confess with our mouths that Jesus is Lord and celebrate our rebirth, but let's not lose the order of it all. Jesus does His work first, we simply respond. In the scientific terms of cause and effect, Jesus is the cause. He acts, we react. Order is significant.

Too many blur this simple truth and have Jesus reacting to us. I've heard many Christians say they are saved because they made the decision to accept Jesus. On the surface that sounds 100 percent correct, but to be a stickler for semantics, the real truth is that there was no decision to be made. We are saved because we accept Jesus, but He did all the work. That's why Paul writes in Ephesians 2:8-9,

> *By grace you have been saved through faith, and that is not of yourselves, it is the gift of God, not of works, lest anyone should boast.*

If getting saved was dependent on us doing something, we might have reason to boast.

Some say that Jesus does the calling, but we still have to decide to answer the door. To that I say, "Nonsense." If Jesus wants us alive, we will be alive. We have no more choice than Lazarus. Besides, if it is we who make the decision to answer the doorbell, then we did something. We would be able to boast. Some could argue that they were smarter than others because they got up from their easy chair and answered the door. Some would say that others are just lazy. But that's not what the Bible says. The

Bible says that life is a gift and we have no room to boast. In Paul's second letter to Timothy, he further writes that it was God

> who has saved us and called us with a holy calling, not according to our works but according to His own purpose and grace which was given to us in Christ Jesus before time began.

God's calling is holy and we will respond.

The Words People Don't Like to Talk About

If you're like I was, you're now saying to yourself, *If God does the calling and He also does the choosing, then that sounds like predestination.* Very few words have the power to divide people and ruffle feathers like the words *predestination* and *election.* Some can't even bring themselves to say the actual words. I've had more than one person ask me if I believe in the "P and E words." I do. But not because I think they're fun and controversial, though I do like to challenge people's thinking on occasion. I believe in them for the same reason you should—they're biblical.

The words *predestination* and *election* are found in dozens of places in Scripture. They're not my words, or words used only by theologians or preachers—they're used repeatedly in the Bible. I won't name all the verses, but one includes Ephesians 1:4-5, in which Paul writes,

> He chose us in Him before the foundation of the world, that we should be holy and without blame before Him in love, having predestined us to adoption as sons by Jesus Christ to Himself, according to the good pleasure of His will.

I particularly like the reference to "before the foundation of the world." That was certainly before we did anything to deserve His favor.

Another passage is 2 Thessalonians 2:13:

We are bound to give thanks to God always for you, brethren beloved by the Lord, because God from the beginning chose you for salvation through sanctification by the Spirit and belief in the truth.

God does the choosing. And Jesus Himself referred to the elect, saying that God "will send His angels with a great sound of a trumpet, and they will gather together His elect from the four winds, from one end of heaven to the other." The elect are those who will inherit eternal life, and they belong to God. Luke also writes in Acts 13:48, "As many as had been appointed to eternal life believed." God does the appointing (ordaining), not us.

The natural argument in response is, "Okay, God chooses, but it's because He knew who would accept Jesus." I thought the same thing for most of my life. I thought God chose based on His foreknowledge of acceptance of His Son. But if God chooses because of something He knew we would do, then it opens the door for boasting. It has God reacting to us. It has God making decisions based on our actions.

I'll cover that further later on, but in a word, God doesn't react to us. God certainly does have foreknowledge of who would accept Jesus, but that's because He wrote the script. It's like an author having foreknowledge of the ending. The author knows the ending because he wrote it. Romans 8:29-30 takes away any argument that foreknowledge and predestination are the same thing. Paul writes, "Whom He foreknew, He also predestined to be conformed to the image of His Son." God foreknew, but He also predestined. They are two separate things.

The Bible Is One Step Ahead of You

I had a real problem with this truth at first. I had a very hard time believing that God chooses some to go to heaven and not others. If we have nothing to do with it, then it becomes very subjective on God's part. He chooses whom He wishes—and there's nothing we can do about it. It doesn't seem fair, and it took me years to come to terms with it, but it's the truth. And you won't hear it in many churches. I can't say I understand any more now than when I first learned of God's election, but I'm humbly thankful for it every day.

And I've come to appreciate the Bible for the definitive place of truth it is. The beauty of the Bible is that it answers every question and anticipates questions as you learn. The apostle Paul taught the hard truth about election in Romans 9, starting with verse 11. Paul is talking there about the twins Jacob and Esau. Though they had not yet been born, nor had they done "any good or evil," God acted as He did so that "the purpose of God according to election might stand, not of works but of Him who calls." Paul goes on to reveal that God loved Jacob but hated Esau. Esau hadn't done anything wrong. He wasn't even born yet, but he was not among God's elect.

I don't understand that any more than you do, but the Bible anticipates your frustration in verse 14: "What shall we say then? Is there unrighteousness with God?" Is God unfair? Keep reading. Verse 14 continues,

Certainly not! For He [God] says to Moses, "I will have mercy on whomever I will have mercy, and I will have compassion on whomever I will have compassion." So then it is not of him who wills, nor of him who runs, but of God who shows mercy.

Paul is explaining election. It's God's decision. It has nothing to do with us. That's a very hard truth to understand, especially in today's take-responsibility, get-empowered world. God elects, we respond. It's a matter of order—and the order is significant.

Your next thought might also be exactly as the Bible anticipates. In verse 19 Paul continues "You will say to me then, 'Why does He still find fault? For who has resisted His will?'" It's a fair question. If God does the choosing and we have nothing to do with it, how can He hold us accountable? The answer comes in verses 20-21:

> *O man, who are you to reply against God? Will the thing formed say to him who formed it, "Why have you made me like this?" Does not the potter have power over the clay from the same lump to make one vessel for honor and another for dishonor?*

In other words, it's not for us to understand. God is the potter, and we are the clay. He does with us as He pleases. I don't have more of an answer because the Bible doesn't give us one. God knows what He is doing; He is in charge; and that's that. It may not seem fair or even fathomable to us, but we're not God. We're not in charge.

༼ ᑎᐢ ༽

As much as I may not have all the answers about election, it does keep me thankful and humble. I suspect God's intention was to not explain things further. He wants us to depend on Him and simply be thankful. After all, we are born dead. If left that way, we will get old and die physically as well as spiritually.

If you're reading this right now and you haven't yet accepted Jesus as your Lord and Savior, I suspect something is going on inside you—else you wouldn't be reading this right now. If you *have* accepted Jesus as your Lord and Savior, stop and give Him thanks right now for intervening in your life. You were dead—and dead people can't help themselves. But He stepped in and called you out of your tomb, as He did with Lazarus, and He gave you eternal life. One of my all-time-favorite passages is Ezekiel 34:11: "Thus says the Lord GOD: 'Indeed I Myself will search for My sheep and seek them out.'" God does the seeking. God does the calling. God does the redeeming. We become born again and then experience faith in Jesus, not the other way around. It's a matter of giving credit where credit is due. It's a matter of order, and order matters.

4

The Ten Commandments Were Not Given to Be Kept

You know the old saying, "Rules were meant to be broken," but you probably have no idea just how biblical that saying really is. Rules are indeed meant to be broken—and the Ten Commandments are no exception. That's not to say they aren't good guidelines on how to conduct your life. They are. But their underlying purpose—the main reason they were given in the first place—is an entirely different matter.

Regardless of their religious faith or denomination, most people admire the Ten Commandments. They've been in the news a lot lately as well. Remember the big flap in Alabama about the monument of the Commandments being displayed on government grounds? That debate is being replayed in almost every state and municipality. Most Christians seem to fall on the side of wanting the Ten Commandments displayed. One prominent pastor told me he wouldn't even want to live in a world where people didn't follow the Ten Commandments. I think I agree. They are God's law and of course we should follow them.

However, following them was never God's intention. It is certainly good for the world's rule of order that we follow them, but God's purpose in giving us His law (not only the Ten Commandments but His other laws as well) is threefold.

1. The law is the vehicle God put in place to judge the world of unbelievers.

2. It is the vehicle God uses to show us our need for a savior.

3. It is the vehicle God uses to point us to Jesus.

Let's look at each one of these purposes much more closely.

A Measuring Stick for Right and Wrong

First, the Ten Commandments, which from now on I'll refer to as the "law,"[9] were given as a means to judge, both for God to judge human beings and for the world to police and judge itself. (People who believe in Jesus are not under the Mosaic law, but under a new law. More on that later in this chapter.) The law is God's measuring stick. It is God's decree, which must be followed to a T, as we discussed in chapter 2. All human beings who are outside of Christ will be judged under the law.[10] There's no wiggle room. As humans, we either stand responsible for every letter of His law or are driven to faith in Jesus.

An Antidote to Chaos

The judging purpose of the law has several practical applications. First, it serves humanity while we're living in our earthly bodies. It governs us while we're on this side of heaven. Without it, chaos would reign. Look at the prime example, the Ten Commandments:[11]

1. "You shall have no other gods before Me."
2. "You shall not bow down or worship other images or idols."
3. "You shall not take the name of LORD your God in vain."
4. "Remember the Sabbath day, to keep it holy."
5. "Honor your father and your mother."
6. "You shall not murder."
7. "You shall not commit adultery."
8. "You shall not steal."
9. "You shall not bear false witness against your neighbor."
10. "You shall not covet your neighbor's house, wife, servant, nor anything that is your neighbor's."

Whenever I read the Ten Commandments, it always amazes me just how thorough it is. Bearing false witness covers all aspects of lying, even the little white lie you told the other day. Coveting is wanting—and any time you've ever wanted something that didn't belong to you, you've broken a commandment. If you've done something contrary to what your mother and father instructed you, you're guilty. The Ten Commandments are a work of genius. Only God could have been the author.

Almost every law ever written by man has at least some of its roots in one of the commandments. Our government considers it illegal to murder, steal, and lie under oath. These laws apply to everyone regardless of religious beliefs and denomination. You violate them and you're going to jail. Even the commandments that may not be illegal to our government are accepted as common law decency and just living. Further, we need to know our boundaries. It would be completely unfair and unjust to be judged without telling us what is required first. Laws are written so that we can never cry foul. Law keeps everyone on an equal playing field and keeps us all from running amuck. God aside, the Ten Commandments are a good governing vehicle for all of us.

A Window on God's Point of View

The other application of the law as judge is so that we know right from wrong from God's perspective. Without law, things are unclear and subjective. God had to give His law so we would know what He expects from us. Paul writes in Romans 4:15, "Where there is no law there is no transgression." In 5:13, he goes a bit further: "Until the law sin was in the world, but sin is not imputed when there is no law." In other words, without the law, accounts of right and wrong aren't kept. We wouldn't know what is right or

> My kids try to find loopholes in the system all the time. When they get in trouble, they often use the defense, "But you never told me not to do that!"...God's law, however, is clear. He has left nothing to chance.

wrong except for the law. Paul tells us in Romans 3:20 that by the law is the knowledge of sin. Right and wrong had to be defined.

Our entire court system is based on defining law. If someone is charged with a crime that is not defined as such, he must be set free. Congress is continually updating, rewriting, and adding new laws so wrongdoers can't escape being judged. My kids try to find loopholes in the system all the time. When they get in trouble, they often use the defense, "But you never told me not to do that!" Sometimes they have a point, and other times they are clinging to a technicality. Sometimes I must amend my own rules to make myself clearer. God's law, however, is clear. He has left nothing to chance. We know what is right and what is wrong because He has told us, and He will hold us accountable. The law was given as a vehicle to judge us, in both the world's eye and God's eye.

Come Out with Your Hands Up

You're probably wondering how I go from validating the law's value to suggesting that the Ten Commandments were not given to be kept. Well, part of the answer is found in deductive reasoning. Psalm 130:3 tell us, "If you, LORD, should count iniquities, who could stand?" The answer is a loud and resounding, "No one!" As we've explored earlier, no one can fully keep the law. It must be kept in thought, word, and deed. It's humanly impossible because we are human. Jesus noted this in Mark 10:18 and Luke 18:19 in His dealings with the rich young ruler, telling him that no one is perfect except God. So there must be another purpose for the law other than merely as a means to judge. If the law was only given as a means to judge and convict us, then that would be pretty hopeless. Thankfully, God doesn't work that way.

That brings us to the second purpose of the law, which is

to drive us to surrender. God continually uses the law to teach us about and remind us of our iniquities and our hopelessly imperfect state. In addition to the Ten Commandments, there are countless other commands God sets forth in Scripture. Among them are, in no particular order, resist the devil, pray without ceasing, abstain from all appearance of evil, don't judge, give your money cheerfully, don't be envious, don't gossip, love your wives, submit to your husband, don't lose your temper, be kind and gentle, be patient. And this is just to name a few. No doubt you can think of many others.

Are you depressed and exhausted yet? Feeling hopeless? If your answer is yes, then it's a good thing. As believers, even though we think we understand the grace of God, the exhortations from the Word often create extreme discomfort in us. This is God's plan. It is through those times of discomfort and helplessness and the times in which we sin that God teaches us the greatest lessons. To put it another way, it's through the times we don't keep the law that we learn and lean on God the most. Sin reminds us we need God.

I've often identified with Paul's pleading with God to remove the thorn in his life. Paul called it "a messenger of Satan to buffet me, lest I be exalted above measure."[12] Paul understood the purpose of the thorn was to keep him humble. Sin is like a thorn or splinter in our life that constantly reminds us to turn to God. God wants us to learn and lean on Him. And He'll do whatever He needs to do to get us to that point—the point of surrender. He wants to break us.

It's puzzling to me, but I guess it's human nature, that when things are going great, I think of God the least. But throw in a crisis or two and I'm turning to God in a second. One person I met in my travels told me he doesn't want to keep turning to God all the time. He said he thought it was a sign of weakness. He went on to tell me that God likes it when he's able to handle things on his own. That attitude couldn't be further from the truth. It's a much weaker position to try to handle things on your own. It's a much stronger position to trust and lean on God.*

He Wants Us to Be Looking at Him

God wants us to look to Him all the time, and He uses the law to conform, mold, and even chastise us when necessary. It's not out of cruelty or because He likes to flex His muscles—it's out of love. One of the most encouraging passages of the entire Bible is found in Hebrews 12:5-6:

> *My son, do not despise the chastening of the* LORD, *nor be discouraged when you are rebuked by Him; for whom the* LORD *loves He chastens, and scourges every son whom He receives.*

The law is the vehicle God uses to scourge us sometimes. At times, it is necessary to remind us of right and wrong and to bring us back in line. He uses the law to force us to surrender and get us to the point of brokenness. This is part of His plan.

I believe God knows what circumstances are essential for each one of us, individually, to surrender. The patriarch Job is the perfect picture of ultimate pressure being applied. Job's circumstances were not thrust upon him because of his sins, but rather to reveal

---

* One of the biggest myths of life is that God helps those who help themselves. In fact, many believe that statement to be in the Bible, but it's not. Ben Franklin was its author, and he wasn't even a believer. He was a deist who did not believe in original sin or our need for a savior. Like many of Ben's sayings and writings, it became accepted as truth. I hope to write a follow-up book on the myths people believe that aren't grounded in Scripture, and I want to call it *7 Popular Beliefs You Won't Find in the Bible!* You can bet the notion that God helps those who help themselves will be included.

God's sovereignty over all our circumstances. Surrendering to Him as Lord over all is His ultimate goal. I recently fell in love with a new song by an up-and-coming Christian country artist called "Canyon Prayer," which sums up the battle of total surrender. If you haven't heard that song yet, consider it a homework assignment to find it. The song is a prayer surrendering control to God. In one line I especially love the singer tells God to go ahead and do what He has to do—to put us through whatever he has to in order to get us to turn to Him.

God uses the law and any other means He deems necessary to cause us to turn to Him. He didn't give us the Ten Commandments because He thought we could keep them; He gave us the Ten Commandments because *we* thought we could keep them. God wants us to surrender to Him—and He uses the law as a means to make that happen.

Rules Made to Be Broken

With that in mind, let's look at how God uses the law to help facilitate surrender. As if following the law wasn't tough enough, catch this—the law even entices us to sin. The mere presence of the law often causes us to stumble. The law encourages us to do wrong. Now, I know that sounds crazy, but think about it. When my son was little, he was a very curious child to say the least. On several occasions, we made the mistake of telling him we had hidden a package of cookies, and once he ate his dinner, he could have a cookie. Well, he would just about go nuts. The second we'd turn our backs on him, he'd be in full hunt mode. He could not rest until he found the cookies. And most of the time, he did. Of course he was punished, but that didn't seem to matter. He had to have the cookies. The truth is, if we hadn't ever told him about the cookies in the first place, he never would have gotten in trouble. Once he knew, he was compelled to break our rule.

The law is like that. Tell someone they can't do something, and they'll do everything in their power to do it. Take Adam and Eve for example. God gave them paradise. They had only one simple rule—and yet they couldn't follow it. Rules produce rebellion, and the Ten Commandments are no exception. Paul tells us this very thing in Romans 7:5:

> *When we were in the flesh, the sinful passions which were aroused by the law were at work in our members to bear fruit to death.*

The law arouses us to sin. It's a temptress. Need more proof? Look at 1 Corinthians 15:56: "The strength of sin is the law." It's the law that entices us to sin. In Romans 5:20 we read, "The law entered that the offense might abound." The law entered so that we'd sin even more! It's clear God gave us the law to drive us to our knees—to the point of surrender. It's like He wanted us to just throw up our hands and say uncle.

It's funny that when I was growing up, the kids who got in the most amount of trouble were kids who grew up in the strictest homes. It seemed like the more rules a kid had, the more determined he or she was to break them. The most promiscuous girls I knew went to all-girls parochial schools. I know that's a big generalization and isn't true all the time, but it seemed like that to me. The more confined and bound we are to rules, the more we look for ways to break free. It doesn't seem fair, but I'll bet you can give countless examples of your own. God wants us to see our own inability to measure up and finally reach the point of surrender. He gave us His law to judge us and to entice us to sin at the same time. Through this He reveals our hopeless humanness!

Getting Headed in the Right Direction

Now, all this seems like a setup, of course. In cop shows, we'd call this a frame job. Is God setting us up? Is God running a divine sting operation? Well, in a way He is. But why? The answer can be found in the third purpose of the law, which is best described in Galatians 3:24:

> *The law was our tutor to bring us to Christ, that we might be justified by faith.*

There it is, the pot of gold at the end of the rainbow. Sure, God uses the law to judge, rebuke, remind, and drive us to surrender—but it's all to lead us to Jesus. The law teaches us of our own inadequacy. The law exposes sin and gets us to the place where we must ask for help. Think of the law as a giant road sign with flashing directional arrows that point straight to Christ.

Let me now complete the verse I started on the previous page. Romans 5:20-21 reads entire,

> *The law entered that the offense might abound. But where sin abounded, grace abounded much more, so that as sin reigned in death, even so grace might reign through righteousness to eternal life through Jesus Christ our Lord.*

The law led to increased sin. But as much as it might have increased, grace increased even more. The more we sin and recognize our helplessness, the more we recognize we need a Savior.

Picture yourself walking down the long road of life. You're tired, weary, defeated, and beat up. Your body aches for rest. Then suddenly you see a sign that says, *Come inside and relax for a while. Free food and drink. Stay as long as you'd like.* That's Jesus. In fact, He said almost that very thing in Matthew 11:28-30:

Come to Me, all you who labor and are heavy laden, and I will give you rest. Take My yoke upon you and learn from Me, for I am gentle and lowly in heart, and you will find rest for your souls. For My yoke is easy and My burden is light.

God gave us His law to lead us straight into the open arms of Jesus Christ.

Escape from the Law

However, it gets even better than that. Once we're in Christ's arms, God wipes away the old law (including the Ten Commandments) and we're not judged by it any longer—at least not by God, anyway. Paul writes of this in Romans 6:14: "Sin shall not have dominion over you, for you are not under law but under grace." He reinforces this later: "Christ is the end of the law for righteousness to everyone who believes" (10:4). Christ is the finishing line as far as the rat race of law is concerned. You are set free. The old law doesn't apply to you. The Ten Commandments have no further purpose for you.

Now, keep in mind that you still live in an earthly society and law is still the rule of order, but as far as God is concerned, you've passed the test. The grade is already entered, and we're on to our next assignment. For that, God has given us a new law to follow. But this time He hasn't left anything to chance. This new law isn't written on stone tablets like the Ten Commandments. It is written on our hearts.[13] This is the same new law that was prophesied by Jeremiah in Jeremiah 31:31-33 and written about again by Paul in Romans 2:15 and 3:27.

In Romans 3:27, Paul calls this new law the law of faith. The old law leads to death; the new law leads to life. The Bible even refers to the old law as "the ministry of death" (2 Corinthians 3:7). The old law is the law that can and will be broken. It was broken in the garden and has been every day since. The new law, the one written in our hearts, can never be broken. Jeremiah calls this new law "a new covenant"—a promise. It's this new law that God had in mind when He gave us the old law—"the ministry of death." He wanted us to surrender and turn to Him. Salvation can't be earned by keeping the law because it is impossible for us to do. Jesus alone fulfilled the law perfectly and conquered the consequences of breaking the law, which is death. And God had this plan for Jesus in mind from the beginning.

∿

My very favorite passage in the entire Bible (I reserve the right to have many "favorite" passages) is the one that makes it clear Jesus was part of God's plan all along. Revelation 13:8 tells us that the Lamb (Jesus) was slain "from the foundation of the world." Before the world was created, before Adam and Eve ever sinned, before the Ten Commandments were given, before anyone knew right from wrong, God had planned the final chapter. He had it all planned before anything happened.

He not only knew what would happen, but had it all figured out. He let sin enter the world, and then He gave His law. He draws us to His Son by revealing our need to be rescued. Augustine once wrote, "God has given us commands that we cannot perform in order that we might know what to ask of Him." As believers, our only response is to confess the weakness of our flesh and rely on the strength given to us through Jesus. This, then, is the purpose of the law. It was not given to be kept, but rather to set up His rescue mission. God's purpose was always Jesus.

5 What You See in the Mirror Is Not the Real You

As with the chicken and the egg in a previous chapter, another question comes to mind—which part of you is most responsible for your identity, the inside or the outside? As I ask that question, the first thing that pops into my mind is Geraldine, the old Flip Wilson comic character, boasting, "What you see is what you get!" (Yes, I know I'm dating myself.) According to Geraldine, the outside is responsible for your identity. After all, that's the part everyone sees. That's the part others recognize. Like it or not, what you see is what you get!

∽

Well, that proclamation may be true for most of life, but when it comes to your spiritual identity, it is as far from the truth as you can get. Most people, including many Christians, believe that what they see in the mirror is their real self. After all, we only know what we see, and what we see is skin and bones. We see all our physical qualities, both the good and the bad. What we see in the mirror is the only self we know.

But what we see is misleading. What we see is flawed. We're not seeing what God sees. I guess I can sum it up best by reciting a slogan popular in the Christian world. I've seen this saying on bumper stickers, T-shirts, even baseball caps: *Christians aren't perfect, just forgiven.* While I understand the intent of that message, the message itself isn't accurate. It's based on seeing the wrong person in the mirror. Christians *are* forgiven—but as a result of the work of the cross, they are also *perfect.* It's an identity issue, one that is critical to understanding your relationship with Jesus.

Okay, Then—Just Who Am I?

So let's start with the obvious question. If what we see in the mirror is not the real us, who is it we're seeing? That's a great question. Our eyes are not totally playing a trick on us. We're seeing the outer part of the person we used to be. We're seeing *flesh.* When we hear the word *flesh,* we think of skin and bones, and that's true, but when Paul writes about flesh in Romans 7 and 8, he is referring to more than outer physical appearances. He is referring to us humans in our original condition. (We talked about this in the previous chapter.) He is talking about someone who is unsaved.

We're all born in flesh. Flesh gets old and wrinkled and will eventually die. We're born into sin and all its imperfections and blemishes. We're born into flesh, descendents of Adam. For unbelievers, that's where they stay. Unbelievers get their identity from their flesh. They're not completely alone in that, though. The world in general establishes identities based on flesh—based on what we see.

The world does indeed judge a book by its cover. The worldly value system is based on seeing and doing. Our identity is tied to our accomplishments and who the world thinks we are. We exchange business cards with titles on them, we exchange resumes that detail our achievements, we refer to each other by what we do for a living. "Sally's a doctor, Bill's a truck driver, and Michelle is a stay-at-home mom." We identify people by income, where they live, race, ethnic background, and whatever else might be apparent to the eye. We judge people, places, and things based solely on what we see, on what it appears to us.

We're all guilty of it. I've done it hundreds of times. I can't tell you how many times I've walked into a hotel and, within seconds, walked right back out, solely because of how it appeared to me in the lobby. I've judged entire neighborhoods by the appearance of a few lawns. That's how things get labeled. Sometimes the labels are right, and sometimes they are wrong, but the labels are hard to shake.

I am reminded of a story I heard Glenna Salsbury tell one time (although I suspect she's told it a lot more than that)—about a man who buys and moves into a broken-down house and begins to restore it from the inside out. The previous owner had all but destroyed the home, but it was worth salvaging. The new owner works night and day fixing up the inside, one room at a time. To all who might pass by, it seems the old homeowner is still living there. The house still appears to be an absolute wreck. But the old owner isn't there any longer, and the house is on its way to being one of the nicest in the neighborhood, regardless of how it appears on the outside.

That's exactly the way it is for Christians. Christ works from the inside out. The old man who used to live in our bodies doesn't live there anymore. In fact, the Bible uses the same language. The old man (the person we used to be) has died. The words "old man" are used in several places: Romans 6:6, Ephesians 4:22, and Colossians 3:9. In each of these passages, Paul informs us that our old self is gone, replaced by a new man in the image of Jesus. We've inherited a brand-new identity. Let's take a look at each of those passages a little closer.

How New Is "Brand-New"?

Romans 6:6 tells us, "Our old man was crucified with Him [Jesus], that the body of sin might be done away with, that we should no longer be slaves of sin." (In verse 22, Paul tells us that we are now slaves of God, but we'll get to that later.) In Ephesians 4:22, Paul writes,

> You...have been taught...that you put off, concerning your former conduct, the old man which grows corrupt according to deceitful lusts, and be renewed in the spirit of your mind, and that you put on the new man which was created according to God, in true righteousness and holiness.

The old man was evicted. There's a new owner in the house who is righteous and holy. The new owner is Jesus.

Colossians 3:9-10 are my favorite verses about the old man and new man, but we have to start with verse 3 to fully appreciate the meaning. Paul writes there, "You died, and your life is hidden with Christ in God." I love that verse. Something had to die for us to become born again. That something was our old self. It may not be readily apparent to the world, but there's a new owner in your body. The new owner is working from the *inside out.* See, unbelievers live *outside in.* That is, they get their identity from the things on the outside, things we can see—like color, gender, physical attributes, and appearances. Believers, on the other hand, are inside out. We get our identity from who we are on the inside. All believers are the same on the inside. All believers have the same tenant, and that's Jesus.

There have been a few times when I've literally looked into someone's eyes and knew they were a believer. I could see Jesus. Of course, Jesus was the only person who walked the face the earth who could tell if a person was alive inside or not, but the spirit of the "real" you shining through the flesh of the "old" you is often noticeable to others. Maybe this is exactly what Jesus meant when He said in Matthew 6:22, "The lamp of the body is the eye. If therefore your eye is good, your whole body will be full of light." I've known people who claim that they can often tell within seconds of meeting someone whether or not they are a believer. I believe them. It's happened to me. Conversely, there have been a few times I've looked into someone's eyes and they seemed dead as a doornail. If the spirit inside is dead, that too is often noticeable.

So, you may be asking, how does this new birth occur? How does the old man die? Well, the old man dies when the new man moves in. The new you is a creation of the Spirit through what is referred to as a spiritual circumcision. Think about that one for a minute. A circumcision is a surgical procedure whereby flesh is cut away from the penis. It's a cutting and discarding procedure. Now let's look at what the Bible says. In Colossians 2:11, Paul writes,

*In Him you were also circumcised with the circumcision made
without hands, by putting off the body of the sins of the flesh,
by the circumcision of Christ.*

In other words, Christ invades your body and cuts away the
dead part and replaces it with His living Spirit. Christ performs a
spiritual circumcision.

This is clear when we read Ezekiel 36:26-27:

*I will give you a new heart and put a new spirit within you; I
will take the heart of stone out of your flesh and give you a new
heart of flesh. [Here this means a heart that is responsive to
God.] I will put My Spirit within you and cause you to walk in
My statutes, and you will keep My judgments and do them.*

We'll chat about what God means when He says He will cause
us to walk in His statutes later on, but for now, let's just focus
on the work He performs within us. Being born again is not just
a metaphor for what happens in us. We are literally *born again*.
God takes out our heart of stone (the one we were born with) and
replaces it with a new one, one that knows, loves, and follows
Jesus. This is how the old man dies and the new man (the new,
real you) is born.

A Conflict Begins with the New Identity

The upshot of all this is that the "real you" is no longer flesh
and bones. The "real you" is the spirit inside. You see the old
you when you look in the mirror, but God sees the image of His
Son, who dwells inside. God sees perfection. He doesn't see the
broken-down, weathered, tired form that is our flesh.

Unfortunately, we can't escape our flesh. That's what we see every time we look in the mirror. We see our old, tired, dying bodies. But this should be reassuring in a strange sort of way. It should be reassuring because Jesus told us that if we believe in Him, we will never die.[14] But we know our bodies die. We're reminded of this every day if we watch the news or read a newspaper. Is it just unbelievers who are dying? Of course not—everyone's body dies. However, when believers' bodies die, these believers are instantly united with Christ and never experience the painful, eternal dying that unbelievers will endure. The spirit of unbelievers will live forever as well—but they will experience true death, which is the painful separation from God for eternity.

So when Jesus tells us that those who believe in Him will never die, He is talking about the spirit you. The real you, not your body, will never die. In heaven you'll get a new body, one that doesn't get sick and old like the one we must live in here on Earth. But for now we're stuck with (rather, stuck inside) our outer, dying flesh.

> **Our identity is not in our flesh, yet that is what we see in the mirror every day. If we don't understand that what we see is not our true identity, it's easy to get depressed and feel like God is against us.**

This, of course, creates a conflict between what you and the world see and what God sees. He may see perfection, but all we see is the sin that is inherent in our fleshly bodies. Our identity is not in our flesh, yet that is what we see in the mirror every day. If we don't understand that what we see is not our true identity, it's easy to get depressed and feel like God is against us.

Paul wrote of this very dilemma in Romans 7:17-23. Let's start with verse 17: "Now, it is no longer I who do it, but sin that dwells in me." That's an interesting statement. Some might argue it's just a classic case of denial, but Paul understands that his identity is not in his flesh. Sin does dwell in his earthly body, but that's not him. He's the new creation inside. That's the part that is redeemed. That's the part that was born again. He's not in denial—he's in Christ!

Paul goes on to lament that the good he wants to do, he doesn't do, and the evil he doesn't want to do, he does do. He's literally at war with his body. It reminds me of the old movie with Steve Martin and Lily Tomlin, *All of Me*. Steve Martin's character occupied one half of his body and Lily Tomlin's occupied the other. They were at odds over everything. One would want to do one thing; the other wanted something completely different. I recall one scene where Martin cried out for help. He wanted to escape Tomlin, but he couldn't. In Romans 7:24, Paul does the same thing. He cries out, "O wretched man that I am! Who will deliver me from this body of death?" The good-news answer follows in verse 25: "I thank God—through Jesus Christ our Lord!" Jesus rescued us from our old selves and gave us a new identity in Him. The old sinner has died and a new saint has been born. You may not feel like a saint, but that's exactly who you are.

Understanding Both Sides—The Inside and the Outside

Let's look at a few more passages to further understand this truth. First, Romans 8:8-9:

Those who are in the flesh cannot please God. But you are not in the flesh but in the Spirit, if indeed the Spirit of God dwells in you. Now if anyone does not have the Spirit of Christ, he is not His.

That is pretty clear. *You* are not your flesh. You *have* flesh. You still must operate *in* flesh, but that's not you. Your flesh will still sin, but that's not who you are anymore. You are a righteous, perfect, saint.

Are you a bit confused? Look at 1 Corinthians 6:9-11:

> *Do you know that the unrighteous will not inherit the kingdom of God? Do not be deceived. Neither fornicators, nor idolaters, nor adulterers, nor homosexuals, nor sodomites, nor thieves, nor covetous, nor drunkards, nor revilers, nor extortioners will inherit the kingdom of God. And such were some of you. But you were washed, but you were sanctified, but you were justified in the name of the Lord Jesus and by the Spirit of our God.*

Isn't that a glorious truth? We used to be sinners, but now we're perfect in God's eyes. We've been washed. We've been justified and sanctified. Look further at 2 Corinthians 5:17: "If anyone is in Christ, he is a new creation; old things have passed away; behold, all things have become new." Our new identity is *in Christ,* regardless of what we may see and feel at any given moment.*

If our identity was in our flesh, we wouldn't feel guilty or remorseful when our bodies sin. Flesh sins, and it doesn't feel guilty about it. We feel guilty because that's not us! We don't have a sin nature any longer, and as a result, we want to repent.[15] Repentance is the Spirit inside agreeing with you, saying, "Yes, that is sin you see in the flesh." The Spirit inside will always be repulsed by sin, and His repulsion produces guilt and remorse. Confessing the sins of the flesh makes us feel better.

Often we also ask for forgiveness, but confessing and asking for forgiveness are not the same thing. It's important to understand

---

* The phrase "in Christ" appears in the New Testament 77 times in the King James Version and 93 times in the New King James Version.

that we've already been forgiven. All of our sins died with our former selves on the cross with Jesus. Galatians 2:20 says it best:

> *I have been crucified with Christ; it is no longer I who live, but Christ lives in me; and the life which I now live in the flesh I live by faith in the Son of God, who loved me and gave Himself for me.*

That sums it all up. Your old self died with Christ on the cross, and now you're a new person with Christ living in you. The Spirit will make us aware of sin and convict us, not to condemn and make us feel guilty, but to keep us humble and to remind us of our true identity. Because there is "no condemnation to those who are in Christ Jesus,"[16] we don't need to fear any condemnation from God on account of our fleshly sins—because our identity has been changed. We're more than forgiven; we're a new person, literally and figuratively.

Really Good News

The significant part of this truth is coming to the realization God will not love us any more than He already does. God does not love us because of what we've done or will do, but because of *who* we are. The love we have for our own children is a good analogy for this. We love our children unconditionally. They may do a lot of things we don't like or condone, but they'll always be our children. It's inescapable. We may love other people's children like our own, but it's not the same. If another person's child does something we don't like, we might not have the same love for that child. That's not the case for our own. We love our children not for what they've done, but simply for who they are. They are ours.

Similarly, we are God's. But as strong as our relationship may be with our children, our relationship with God is even deeper. In fact, it goes beyond a relationship. We *belong* to Him. He bought us. In 1 Corinthians 6:20 we read, "You were bought at a price." Of course, we know that price was Jesus dying on the cross, but that means we belong to Him. Verse 17 in the same chapter tells us we've become "one spirit with Him." That's not a close *relatio*nship—that's *one*-ship! That's *connected*-ship! Even children can separate themselves from their parents, but we can never separate ourselves from God. God did more than redeem us from sin; He united us to Himself through His Son. We are one with Him. Our identity is *in Christ*. We're not separate people, nor can we be separated. As always, the Bible says it best:

> *We are more than conquerors through Him who loved us. For I am persuaded that neither death nor life, nor angels nor principalities nor powers, nor things present nor things to come, nor height nor depth, nor any other created thing, shall be able to separate us from the love of God which is in Christ Jesus our Lord.*

That's from Romans 8:37-39, the cornerstone passage for peace and security in our new identity.

To borrow a page from author Steve McVey's *Grace Walk* workbook,

> *Most Christians seem to have a spiritual inferiority complex. In spite of the fact that God speaks highly of His children, they have a low opinion of themselves. Their perception of their identity is*

that they have been saved by God's grace, but that they are still basically just sinners who are trying with God's help to live the kind of lifestyle He wants them to live. Do you see yourself as a saved sinner who tries to serve God to the best of your ability? That description falls short of God's perception of those who have come to Him through Christ.

Let's not live as if God is some distant entity waiting to welcome us to His kingdom when we die. With Christ moved in, we're a resident of the kingdom of God—we're a part of His family. It doesn't get any better than that! You're not waiting for your inheritance; you already have it. So stop living as if someday, maybe, if you play your cards right, you'll be one with Jesus. You already are! You are not the person you see in the mirror. You are a new creation—one who belongs to God, one who is united in spirit with Him, one who has the mind of Christ,[17] one who cannot be separated from the love of God, one who has peace in knowing *who* they really are.

6

Trying to Live for Jesus Will Only Frustrate You

The concept of "living for Jesus" in the sense of trying to do as Jesus would do can—and often does—produce a life of real frustration. The phrase *WWJD* (What Would Jesus Do?) has become a pop icon, but trying to live for or even like Jesus is like the tail wagging the dog.

The problem lies in the two words *trying* and *for*. I'll tackle the issue of *trying* versus *trusting* later in this chapter, but it's either one or the other. Equally, living *for* Jesus is not what God has in mind for the Christian life. On the other hand, living *with* Jesus is empowering and uplifting. And allowing Jesus to live *through* us is the very essence of what it means to be a Christian. As believers, Christ is in us. His life is perfect, holy, and pleasing to the Father.

We no longer live, but rather Christ lives in us (see Galatians 2:20). We cannot become "holier" by striving to please God. This is only accomplished through His Son.

To further understand the truths of this chapter we must come to grips with *trying* and *for*. You might think I'm just playing with semantics, but those two little words hold the key to greater peace and rest. Bottom line: God doesn't depend on us for help, and He doesn't need our help.

Surely I've Got Something to Offer!

First, let's tackle the issue of whether or not God depends on us to accomplish His work. It is important to remember here the condition into which we were born. We were born spiritually dead. God intervened, with no help from us, and made us alive. We were saved by grace. We covered all this earlier. We didn't do anything to earn God's favor, nor did we do anything to assist God in our salvation. Salvation is of the Lord.[18] Why is it that we readily accept being saved by grace, but once we're saved, we believe there's a whole host of things we now must do?

I recently had dinner with a couple who openly boasted in the fact they were working for the Lord. They wore it like a badge of honor. Their work was impressive. They volunteered tirelessly in their church and had been on several mission trips. Both taught Sunday school and were active in Bible studies within their community. (All things I commend, I might add.) What I don't commend is the reasons for their efforts. The wife told me her work was to please God, to gain His favor. The husband said it was a small way to try to repay God.

Both are off the mark, though. Let's start with the wife's remark about trying to gain favor. If we can gain favor by our works, where does grace fit in? Paul wrote of this extensively throughout the New Testament. Much of the book of Galatians is Paul chastising the believers in Galatia, who were trying to be "good Christians" through outward obedience, self-effort, and law-keeping. Paul wrote them, "Are you so foolish? Having begun in the Spirit, are you now being made perfect by the flesh?"(3:3). To put it another way, if you already have Christ in you, why go backwards and try to be more perfect on your own? Is not Christ enough?

In Romans 4:2-4 Paul writes,

If Abraham was justified by works, he has something to boast about, but not before God. For what does the Scripture say? "Abraham believed God, and it was accounted to him for righteousness." Now to him who works, the wages are not counted as grace but as debt.

That makes sense. Think about it. If you work outside the home and receive a paycheck, do you thank your boss when he or she hands you your money? Not necessarily. In fact, you might even grumble under your breath that your boss is not paying you enough. You don't thank your boss because your paycheck isn't a favor. You earned it.

That's what Paul is talking about. To him or her who works for favor, it isn't grace. It's a debt. In other words, if we can work to earn God's favor, He would owe us. He would be in debt to us! Paul is even clearer in Romans 11:6, saying that if God's choosing comes "by grace, then it is no longer of works; otherwise grace is no longer grace. But if it is of works, it is no longer grace; otherwise work is no longer work." Grace and works are diametrically opposed. It can't be both. The gift of eternal life, our salvation itself, is free. There can be no boasting in that (Ephesians 2:8). The same truth prevails in our daily walk as believers. We're saved by grace; we live by grace.

Maybe God Deserves a Tip?

As for the husband's comment about wanting to repay God, that may seem noble—but can you really even begin to repay God for what He has done? Should we even try? Is not any attempt to repay Him an insult to Him? We need only look to the story of Mary and Martha in Luke 10:38-42. Mary sat at Jesus' feet and listened intently to all He had to say while Martha was busy trying to serve Him. Jesus praised Mary and basically told Martha to chill out. When you endeavor to serve and live for Jesus, it's a never-ending, never-resting proposition. You've heard the advertising slogan, "Be like Mike." Well, God wants you to "Be like Mary" and rest at the feet of Jesus. Any attempt to repay Him will fall woefully short.

For more on this, turn to the parable of the invited wedding guests in Luke 14:7-14. Jesus was using a parable to show us it's better to be humble, grateful, and accepting of grace than to seek to repay such goodness. I particularly like verse 11: "Whoever exalts himself will be humbled, and he who humbles himself will be exalted." Any attempt to repay God is elevating ourselves to a level that is unwarranted and unachievable. My first thought when my friend told me he was trying to repay God was that of caution. God has a way of humbling us when we think too highly of ourselves. Charles Spurgeon, the great preacher of the nineteenth century, says it best:

God accomplishes His plan by His own unaided omnipotence. If

He speaks, it is done—done by Himself. He doesn't depend upon the cooperation of the puny strength of men.[19]

Hey, God—At Least I Could Hand You the Tools...

Now, here is another shocking reality. God doesn't even want us to *try* to live the Christian life! Now, before you throw this book down, bear with me. The term or concept of the "Christian life" is man-made. Even the term *Christian* wasn't coined until long after Jesus' life on Earth. The term was first used some decades later, and it was a way to label people more than anything else.

So here's the million-dollar question we touched on earlier: Why is it that as believers we readily accept we are saved by grace and grace alone, but then we begin to try to live the Christian life? It's worth asking again—if we could not "help" ourselves become saved, what makes us think we can now "help" Him accomplish His work in us? Does grace go out the window once we become a Christian? We readily accept and believe (and rightly so) that we didn't do anything to merit eternal life on our own, that salvation is not based on any works—so why is it that many believe the rules change once we become a Christian?

The truth is, the rules don't change. God saved us by grace, and He wants us to live by grace. In his amazing book *The Pleasures of God*, John Piper writes,

> *So often you find in many churches and ministries the cultivation of an implicit two-stage Christianity: a faith stage and then (maybe) an obedience stage. But this is not the way the Bible pictures the life of faith. The separation of faith and obedience, as though faith were necessary for salvation and obedience were optional, is a mistake owing to a misunderstanding of what faith really is. True saving faith is not the kind of belief in the*

facts of the gospel that leaves the heart and life unchanged. If it were, then God's pleasure in obedience would indeed be bad news. He would be saying that we are saved by faith, and then, to please Him with obedience, we must move beyond faith to something else in order to produce good behavior. This is not good news. The good news is that saving faith is by its nature a life-changing power.[20]

As Piper explains, God supplies the transforming power necessary to sustain us in grace. It's inherent in our identity in Christ. The power is Christ Himself.

Look at 2 Thessalonians 2:16-17 to better understand where our faith-sustaining power comes from: "May our Lord Jesus Christ Himself, and our God and Father, who has loved us and given us everlasting consolation and good hope by grace, comfort your hearts and establish you in every good word and work." God establishes our every good word and work. Our job is to take comfort in that and give Him the glory. Our very obedience comes as a result of God's Spirit working in us. It is not something we do ourselves. We can't muster up obedience, nor can we take any credit for it.

Credit Where Credit Is Due

In 2 Corinthians 12:9, Paul informs us of this truth outright:

He said to me, "My grace is sufficient for you, for My strength is made perfect in weakness." Therefore most gladly I will rather boast in my infirmities, that the power of Christ may rest upon me.

Note what Paul is saying. He is responding to Christ in grace. Jesus said that His grace is sufficient, and Paul humbly accepted this. The apostle didn't try to say, "Yeah, thanks for Your grace—but now it's my turn to do for You." Rather, he said he would most gladly boast in weakness and rest in the power of Christ.

When man is weak, Christ is strong, thus making man strong. When man tries to be strong and live out of self-effort, the net effect is weakness. Paul concluded in 2 Corinthians 12:10, "When I am weak, then I am strong." That can only make sense if we are resting in the power of God's grace. If we think that through our own self-effort and discipline that we are capable of living the Christian life, this is a weak and even dangerous position. It's potentially dangerous because even if we are somewhat successful in being outwardly obedient, we often become proud of our performance and in turn can become very judgmental of those who, in our eyes, are not as obedient. This is boasting, whether verbalized or not.

So you may ask, "How do you know if your obedience is a result of the pride of the flesh or the work of the Spirit?" This is a crucial question. The answer is life-changing. Obedience is always and only possible through the work of the Spirit. It's classic "trying" versus "trusting." You're either trying to achieve it on your own, or you're trusting in God's grace at work in empowering you. These are mutually exclusive. If you're trying, it's of the flesh. If you're trusting, it's of the Spirit.

In Romans 15:18, Paul says, "I will not dare to speak of any of those things which Christ has not accomplished through me, in word and deed, to make the Gentiles obedient." His work in us began by grace and will continue to be by grace. Paul also writes in 1 Corinthians 15:10, "By the grace of God I am what I am, and His grace toward me was not in vain; but I labored more abundantly than they all, yet not I, but the grace of God which was with me." Even though Paul labored, he knew it was not by his own might, but by the might supplied by the grace of God.

That's why grace is so wonderful. As Christians, we sing about grace, we give thanks for grace, we talk a lot about grace, but grace is even more wonderful than we could ever imagine. God doesn't want us to take one ounce of credit for living the Christian life. He doesn't want to share His glory. "He who glories, let him glory in the Lord."[21]

"Helping God Get Things Done"

The other aspect of "trying to live for Jesus" revolves around the issue of whether God "needs" our help. I ran into a young youth minister who described living for Jesus as "helping God accomplish the things He needs to get done." It immediately reminded me of the old bumper sticker that reads, *God Is My Co-Pilot*. My young friend's enthusiasm was admirable, yet his basic assumption was wrong. I reminded him it was only by grace that we are even passengers in coach, let alone co-pilots!

Together we looked at Acts 17:25: "Nor is He worshiped with men's hands, as though He needed anything, since He gives to all life, breath, and all things." We then looked at Philippians 2:13, which clearly says that *God* does the work in us. With some visible signs of relief, this young man confessed that maybe his view of God had been too small.

This is not uncommon. Most people would not argue about the ultimate power of God, yet they live their lives as if God wasn't big enough to handle their day-to-day affairs. We'll explore the complete sovereignty of God later, but for now let's just say that God is in charge of everything. Look at Colossians 1:16 whenever you need to be reminded of this:

By Him all things were created that are in heaven and that are on earth, visible and invisible, whether thrones or dominions or principalities or powers. All things were created through Him and for Him.

Sounds like a legal document that attempts to cover all the bases. God wanted to cover all His bases in letting us know He's in charge.

Many Christians mistakenly believe that even though God is in control, it is still up to us to accomplish His plan for our lives. In other words, God needs us to cooperate in order to fulfill His end result. This only leads to further frustration. What if we don't cooperate? What if we don't do as God needed us to do? What if we miss His calling? What if we mess things up for God?

Well, if we could, even inadvertently, mess up God's plan, then I would argue that *we*, not God, are in control. The truth is, God has preordained the paths in which we will walk and will see to it that we walk in them. We can't go contrary to God's plan, and He doesn't need us to make it happen. Let's look at two things: first, the fact that God has preordained our path, and second, that God will guide us on that path. Look again at Philippians 2:13 as the anchor passage for this discussion: "It is God who works in you both to will and to *do* for His good pleasure." I could just end the discussion there, but let's dissect it a little further.

God Had Things Worked Out Before We Came Along

God has a mission for our lives. He not only knows what we will do, He has planned our steps. Wise King Solomon wrote in Proverbs 16:9, "A man's heart plans his way, but the LORD directs his steps." He wrote in Proverbs 16:1, "The preparations of the heart belong to man, but the answer of the tongue is from the

God sought us out and purchased us and placed His Holy Spirit within us to do His will on earth. He isn't sitting back on pins and needles wondering what we might do.

LORD." What he's saying is that we may have plans of our own, but it's the Lord's plans, not ours, that will prevail.

God doesn't redeem us from death only to sit back and see what happens. Think about that for a minute. It's like saving your entire life for a brand-new car, and then—when you finally purchase your dream car—turning the keys over to a friend. God sought us out and purchased us and placed His Holy Spirit within us to do His will on earth. He isn't sitting back on pins and needles wondering what we might do. Paul wrote in Ephesians 2:10, "We are His workmanship, created in Christ Jesus for good works, which God prepared beforehand that we should walk in them." That says a bundle. We are *His* work, not ours, and we were created to do good things. Those good works, whatever they might be, were preordained for us long before we even existed.

Another passage to support this truth is found in Hebrews 13:20-21:

> *May the God of peace who brought up our Lord Jesus from the dead, that great Shepherd of the sheep, through the blood of the everlasting covenant, make you complete in every good work to do His will, working in you what is well pleasing in His sight, through Jesus Christ, to whom be glory forever and ever. Amen.*

That definitively answers the question of obedience we explored earlier in this chapter. Any good works we do are because of God. He ordains them and He performs them.

That also answers the great, mysterious question of the ages—"What is the meaning of life? Why were we created?" We were created to serve God. We were created to do His will. We were created to carry out His plan for us. He has a plan for everyone, and that plan was prepared long ago. There's no need to fret, wondering whether or not God has a plan for us or if we will carry out His plan. He does, and we will. There's no need to worry about it for one second.

Let's look at a few further passages from the Word, starting with 1 Thessalonians 5:23-24:

> *May the God of peace Himself sanctify you completely; and may your whole spirit, soul, and body be preserved blameless at the coming of our Lord Jesus Christ. He who calls you is faithful, who also will do it.*

That passage should produce a huge sigh of relief. It would be cruel of God to bring us to Jesus and then say, "Okay, you're on your own now. Hope you make it to the finish line—and by the way, you need to be blameless when you get there!" Wow—thank You, God, for not doing that! He will preserve us and keep us "blameless" before Him.

And in Ezekiel 36:27, we read, "I will put My spirit [this is God talking] within you and cause you to walk in My statutes, and you will keep My judgments and do them." God will cause us to do what He expects from us. He will absolutely make certain that our spirit, soul, and body will be completely blameless. As we discussed in an earlier chapter, Christ is in us. We are "sealed" with the Holy Spirit, who is our guarantee (Ephesians 1:13-14). It's really very reassuring. We won't miss God's calling, nor will we go astray from it.

Take a Load Off

Understanding what we've been looking at is critical to understanding the truth we began with. Trying to live for Jesus will only frustrate you. If you believe it's up to you, then you are setting yourself up for a life of frustration, disappointment, and condemnation. Unfortunately, many Christians still carry around this burden. They live in a vicious cycle of trying to please God, falling short, begging for forgiveness, and recommitting to trying to do better. Does that sound familiar? It's never-ending for many Christians.

Fortunately, that's not the Christian life. That's bondage. And it's not what Jesus had in mind when He said in Matthew 11:29, "Take My yoke upon you and learn from Me, for I am gentle and lowly in heart, and you will find rest for your souls. For My yoke is easy and My burden is light." Trying is a work of the flesh; trusting is a work of the Spirit. We're either trying or trusting—and I choose trusting God. We don't need to live for Jesus; He will live through us. He will. We don't need to live our lives wondering what God wants from us, or if we've done enough for Him. He just wants *us*. He doesn't want or need our broken promises or self-serving intentions. He doesn't want or need us to live the Christian life. He wants us to rest in His glory. He wants us to find peace in Him.

Some might argue that all this sounds pretty passive, but I'll argue that it's active rest. I have to continually remind myself it's not up to me. Sometimes, it's hard work to strip myself away from the natural human tendencies of the flesh and just trust God. Active rest is anything but passive. It's actively thanking God, giving Him the credit, and expecting Him to live through us. That is the life of faith.

∽

Taking it upon ourselves to work and live for Jesus is self-promoting and works-oriented. Passiveness is doing nothing and calling it fate. Active rest is finding the peace and joy of knowing that the Lord is at work in us and giving Him the credit for everything. There's a big difference between these three: trying, passiveness, and active rest. Rejoicing in God's glory is never passive. Jesus recognized He could not do anything apart from the Father, saying in John 5:30, "I can of Myself do nothing." He wasn't being passive. He just understood where His power came from, and He was content with that.

Finding that kind of peace and contentment is what the Christian life is really all about. That is actively resting! It's not about working and living for Jesus. It is the Lord Himself who makes us complete in every good work. We can either toil trying to live for Jesus—or rest in His faithfulness.

7 Prayer Doesn't Change God's Mind

While I admit that all my chapter titles have an edgy sound to them, none are nearly as edgy as this one. Prayer is special to the believer, and rightfully so. It is a huge part of the believer's relationship with God.

And I believe in the power of prayer. I just don't believe that prayer changes God's mind. To believe that it does might suggest that prayer, not God, is sovereign. It's a matter of who controls what. Does prayer control God, or does God control prayer? I believe God controls and uses prayer, not the other way around. I find it absurd to believe that the Creator of all things, both visible and invisible,[22] is deciding things based on what we pray or don't pray. I can't imagine God saying, "Wow, that's a pretty good idea. I hadn't thought of that before"—or worse yet, "I wasn't planning on doing that, but hey, why not—you've been a faithful servant."

To me, it's that simple, but more important than what I believe, it's also biblical. God does indeed ordain and use prayer as a means of accomplishing His will, which makes it incredibly important—but it doesn't make prayer sovereign. Prayer is a tool God uses to accomplish His plans. He isn't deciding what happens on the fly, based on the prayers of man.

A God-Designed Process of Discovery

So let's begin by examining what prayer is and isn't. The average person would define prayer as the means by which we communicate with God, and that would be accurate. Prayer is a way of talking to God, but it's much more than that. It's also the way we listen to and get in step with God as well. My friend Glenna Salsbury has the very best definition of prayer I've ever heard: "the *process* of discovering what the Lord is doing and coming alongside Him in that."

By "coming alongside," she means sensing what the Lord's will is and praying accordingly. (I particularly love the word *process*.)

Let's look at what the Bible has to say about prayer in Romans 8:26:

> *The Spirit also helps in our weaknesses. For we do not know what we should pray for as we ought, but the Spirit Himself makes intercession for us with groanings which cannot be uttered.*

Prayer is the *process* of discovering what the Spirit already knows. His "groanings" can best be understood as His rephrasing of our requests to comply with God's highest and best for us. Going along with this, 1 Thessalonians 5:17 reads, "Pray without ceasing." This is an exhortation, and I believe it is also a fruit of the Spirit. The Spirit in you is always communing with the Father. He doesn't cease. He knows what the Father is doing and is in constant prayer over it. Our job is to trust the Spirit and join Him in that effort. Joining Him is nothing more than trusting Him. James the apostle underscores this: "You ought to say, 'If the Lord wills, we shall live and do this or that'" (James 4:15).

Hitches in Our Way of Communicating

The hitch in the process is that our perception of prayer begins forming at a very young age with something like the old "Now I lay me" prayer. We get trained in the mind-set that prayer involves a specific format and must contain our requests of God. I was taught, as I'll bet some of you were too, to close my eyes, bow my head, fold my hands, get on my knees, and tell God what I needed. "Now I lay me down to sleep, I pray the Lord my soul to keep. If I should die before I wake, I pray the Lord my soul to take." Then I was taught to run through the list of people I wished God to bless. I started with Mommy and Daddy and often concluded with my dogs and the most remote of acquaintances. Prayer was more of a chore and ritual than anything else, but I suspect it was good training for a young child. (I've even taught "Now I lay me" to my children.)

However, there are two potential dangers with teaching prayer this way. The first one is that it perpetuates the notion that prayer requires a certain form and posture. The truth is, prayer doesn't need to happen when you're alone at night on your knees with your eyes closed. Prayer can take place anytime, anywhere. I often pray out loud while I'm driving down the road. I can only imagine what other drivers think when they see me having what they think is a conversation with myself. I also pray without uttering a sound—when people are around me, with my eyes wide open. God hears my thoughts, and I hear His. He hears yours, too! We don't need to put off prayer until all the conditions are just perfect. Prayer can be spontaneous.

The second potential harm lies in the perception that if we petition God long and hard enough, He will grant us our wishes. We recite the same prayer over and over because we sometimes fall into the belief that God will answer our prayers if we are persistent enough. After all, that's what the world teaches us. You know, the old "try and try again" attitude. Often persistence does pay off, so it only makes sense that the same dynamic would work with God.

Pleading with and petitioning God for the things we want or need is unfortunately the way most of us pray, most of the time. Jesus warned the religious leaders of His day about their failure to grasp the true basis for prayer. He said,

> *When you pray, you shall not be like the hypocrites. For they love to pray standing in the synagogues and on the corners of streets, that they may be seen by men...And when you pray, do not use vain repetitions as the heathen do. For they think that they will be heard for their many words* (Matthew 6:5-7).

Rather, Jesus taught us to pray, "Your will be done" (Matthew 6:10). That is, the will of the Father—not ours. Prayer is the means of experiencing His presence and coming into agreement with His will for us.

Interestingly, in Luke 11, the Lord teaches what, on the surface, seems like a contradiction. After He teaches the Lord's Prayer in verses 1 through 4, He then gives the strange example of a person who receives help because he persisted in knocking, requesting help from his neighbor. In His concluding remark in Luke 11:9 and 13, summarizing what He is teaching about prayer, He says,

I say to you, ask, and it will be given to you; seek, and you will find; knock, and it will be opened to you...How much more will your heavenly Father give the Holy Spirit to those who ask Him!

Jesus is telling us that true prayer is to pray without ceasing, expecting the wisdom and power of the Holy Spirit to be given us—but not necessarily the fulfillment of our personal desires or requests!

"Now God, Did You Think About This Point?"

I think it's a natural human tendency to turn to God when things get rough. I mentioned in an earlier chapter how I find myself turning to God more in times of trouble than when things are sailing along wonderfully. When things are going well, we think *we've* got everything under control. That is not what God had in mind. There are two truths that I, and all Christians, need to keep in mind.

First, as I noted, the Spirit is at work intervening all the time. Repeated prayer may help us feel closer to God, but through the Spirit, God already knows our needs and wishes. Jesus explained this in Matthew 6:31-32:

Do not worry, saying "What shall we eat?" or "What shall we drink?" or "What shall we wear?" For after all these things the Gentiles seek. For your heavenly Father knows that you need all these things.

God knows what we need. He knows it before *we* know it.[23] Asking

Him for things in prayer may help us feel like we're being more proactive, but it won't tell God anything He didn't already know. He knows what we need.

He also knows what is best for us. To adapt a line from a famous Garth Brooks song, "Unanswered prayers are some of God's greatest gifts." If God had granted every prayer I've ever made, my life would be a disaster. I'd be married to a different woman, I'd be in a completely different occupation, I wouldn't have the children I have, and I certainly wouldn't be writing this book. Here's a quick personal story to illustrate this point.

I was born David Maiatico in Allentown, Pennsylvania. That's pronounced *my-AT-tico,* a good Italian name. My mother and father divorced when I was three, and I grew up, as many kids do, without a dad. Thankfully, my grandparents pitched in and helped raise me and my sister. My mother worked nights and weekends to support us.

I grew up on the low end of the middle class. My true passion was baseball, and I was able to play only one year of organized Little League because we simply could not afford it. The only fights that ever occurred in my house between my mother and grandmother were over money. When the fights got too intense, I would retreat to the space in my backyard between the shed and the fence. It was there I prayed hundreds of times for God to just make me rich. I prayed earnestly and fervently, incorrectly believing that money was the key to happiness, incorrectly believing I knew what was best for my life.

Well, to jump ahead in the story, when I turned 13 my mother remarried, and the gentleman she married adopted my sister and me. When you're adopted, you are issued a brand-new birth certificate bearing your new last name. This man's last name was—you guessed it—"Rich"...and overnight, I became "Rich." Not exactly what I had prayed for!

The Lord surely has a sense of humor, but it was, of course, the very best thing that could have happened to me. We are all completely unqualified to know what is best for us. We only know what we see and feel at the moment we pray. We don't see the big picture. We can't see the future. We don't know how all the pieces fit together—but thank God, He does. Romans 8:28 tells us, "We know that all things work together for good to those who love God, to those who are called according to His purpose." Yet we often seem to think we know what is best for our lives, and if we just ask God enough times, He will give in to our plans or requests.

"Father, You Really Ought to Reconsider Your Decision Here..."

This leads us to the second issue. Do our repetitious petitions change what God was already planning on doing? The answer is a resounding *no*. Now, petitioning God is indeed one form of prayer, and it's something we should do. In fact, one of the Hebrew words translated *pray* is *beah*, which means *to petition*. The Bible is full of examples of people petitioning God, but it doesn't change or alter His plan. In my case, He had a plan for my life—and it didn't include wealth, despite my desperate pleas. Romans 8:27 reinforces this concept: "He who searches the hearts knows what the mind of the Spirit is, because He makes intercession for the saints according to the will of God." The key part of that passage is "according to the will of God," not according to our will. Wanting or trying to change God's mind is fruitless because the Holy Spirit Himself is pleading for us believers in harmony with God's own will.

The point I am striving to make in this chapter isn't that

prayer isn't important or that it isn't an integral part of the way God accomplishes His will. It is. Always has been and always will be—but it doesn't change God's mind. If prayer could change His mind, then prayer would be sovereign in that it would have power over Him. He is not a reactionary God. As we read in 1 Samuel 15:29, God "will not lie, nor will he change his mind, for he is not human that he should change his mind!" (NLT). God doesn't alter or make up His plans as He goes. That would be counter to Scripture that declares God's work as finished.[24]

God's work is not a work in progress. It's complete. Look at what the Bible says in Daniel 4:35:

> *All the inhabitants of the earth are reputed as nothing; He does according to His will in the army of heaven and among the inhabitants of the earth. No one can restrain His hand or say to Him, "What have You done?"*

What that means is that no one can pray his or her way in or out of God's will. God's plan will be done. It isn't for us to question.

These realities are designed to bring us peace and comfort. Jesus Himself lived in the reliance on the Father's will. One of many such passages that illustrate this can be found in John 6:38: "I have come down from heaven, not to do My own will, but the will of Him who sent Me." It should be comforting to us to know that God, who knows the end from the beginning, can be trusted in regard to His own plan for our lives. And prayer helps us get in touch with what He's doing.

What Would It Be Like If You Could Sway God's Plans?

Let's play "what if?" for a moment. What if prayer were able to change God's mind? Think of the consequences. Think of what an incredible burden that would be to carry around! You wouldn't have the luxury to pray as you were led—you would have an obligation to pray for everyone and everything. People wouldn't be praying in sincere, Spirit-led communication, they'd be praying out of sheer desperation. Prayer would become divine begging. And in today's capitalistic society, you might even see "prayer clinics" where we might fall prey to some who claim they have an inside track with God. Strangers would solicit your prayers, and daily life would be overcome with angst and stress. Selfish prayer would become the norm—and everyone would be trying to persuade God to see things their way.

You might think I'm going a bit overboard, but aspects of this happen now. Let me give you a couple examples. My son went through a series of surgeries a few years ago. We weren't getting many clear answers from his doctors, so a friend of our family called us and told us that if we would "pray hard enough" we would be able to find the answers we were looking for. I'm sure this person meant the phone call as inspiration, but we hung up feeling devastated. What if our son's ongoing condition was because we hadn't prayed enough? What if our prayers weren't "hard" enough? How "hard" was hard enough?

God never intended for us to carry around prayer as a burden—or like a noose around our neck waiting to hang us. Prayer was designed as a means for us to feel closer to God, not as a way of driving a wedge between us and Him.

Thankfully, the feeling of desperation didn't last long because we knew that wasn't how God operated. Whatever happened or happens with my son is in God's plan. Yes, we prayed for different results; however, we rest in what has unfolded because He has a perfect plan. We all plead with Him from time to time for circumstances to be different, but He knows best. When Paul wrote in 2 Corinthians 12:8 about pleading to God three times for the satanic thorn in his flesh to be removed, God's answer to him was basically that He had another plan. The things that unfold in our lives aren't a result of inefficient or insufficient prayers. Things unfold as God would have them!

Another friend once told my wife she hadn't been in "confessional prayer" for quite a while—and if she died before she had a chance to confess her sins in prayer, she might not go to heaven! That's a burden. God never intended for us to carry around prayer as a burden—or like a noose around our neck waiting to hang us. Prayer was designed as a means for us to feel closer to God, not as a way of driving a wedge between us and Him (nor as a means of earning God's favor). God does hear the prayers of believers, and through His Spirit He comforts us—but He doesn't change His mind.[25] He wants us to pray as Jesus prayed. Jesus prayed all the time. But He knew that it wasn't His will, but the Father's will, that would be done.

Thus, we should pray seeking answers, not giving directions. It's natural to petition God for things we think we need, but we'll find greater comfort and assurance if we add the words "if it is Your will" to every prayer. That way, if things work out the way we pray, we can rest in knowing it was God's plan. If things don't work out the way we pray, we can also rest and know it was God's plan. Get it? Either way, it's God's plan. We can either struggle against it, or rest in Him.

So Why Bother?

The obvious next questions—and ones I hear all the time, are, why bother praying at all? And what's the use of intercessory prayer? Let's tackle the latter first.

Intercessory prayer is important for two reasons. First, it bonds and unites believers together. The Bible tells us to pray together, and intercessory prayer is a way of communing. It's empathizing with our fellow believers. It's an intimate way of connecting and one way we can show we care. Jesus commanded us to love our neighbors as ourselves—praying for them is the ultimate expression of love.

The church I attend has an exemplary program of intercessory prayer. It brings us together, and we find peace in being able to lay our problems at Christ's door—which is the second good reason for intercessory prayer. Some might argue that praying for other people's problems only adds anxiety to our already stressful life. That would be correct if we were praying to change God's mind. However, if we are praying "not my will," but God's will, praying for others can be highly therapeutic. Praying for others will release us from the burden rather than intensifying it. We are giving the burden up to God. It is now His problem, not ours. If it's in His plans, it will be done. Either way, intercessory prayer shifts the burden of responsibility to the One to whom it belongs.

If God's Gonna Do What God's Gonna Do...

As for the question of why to bother praying at all—well, if I had a dollar for every time someone used that as rebuttal to truths I'm presenting, I would be wealthy. I could answer that concern in many ways. For instance, I could suggest that a person really doesn't understand prayer in the first place if he or she thinks prayer's primary purpose is to affect God. I could mention all the points I've talked about in this chapter—that we pray because it's a way of feeling closer to God, that it's a way of releasing burdens, a way of getting in touch with what He's doing, or perhaps just a way of saying thanks. Further, prayer is the best way to celebrate Jesus and to say nothing more than thank you. Prayer is a way to praise God, and perhaps that's the best reason for praying in the first place.

But the simplest, most basic argument for prayer all boils down to this: We pray because we're led to pray. There are times I feel absolutely compelled to pray. Sometimes for myself and sometimes for others, but it's a feeling that comes over me that can only be explained by saying it is Spirit-led. His Spirit compels us to pray, preach, witness, do missionary work, and whatever else might be ordained for us. It's good to recall at this point the passage in Ephesians 2:10 we looked at in an earlier chapter:

We are His workmanship, created in Christ Jesus for good works, which God prepared beforehand that we should walk in them.

∼∾

So there you have it. We're led to pray because prayer is one of the means God has ordained to accomplish His will. Prayer is a tool He uses to do His work on earth. His plan is sovereign, and it cannot be foiled or altered. And who among us would want it any other way? Sometimes our prayers are answered the way we want; sometimes they're not; but either way, it is God's will, not ours, that prevails.

There's comfort in that. Prayer is an essential element in the life of a believer, but it's not a magic potion. Nor is there any such thing as fate. Things happen for a reason—and all things are for God's reasons. We may not understand them (see Isaiah 55:8-9), but that's okay. God has everything planned, and He has it all figured out.

Therefore, prayer doesn't change God's mind. It never has and it never will, but that won't stop us from praying. We will pray because the Spirit will lead us to do so. We have the privilege of entering into God's work through "the process." Prayer is coming alongside Him in His purpose. And when all is said and done, our only response can be a loud, joyful *amen*.

God Keeps Satan on a Leash

I wish I were a fly on the wall so I could hear what you're saying to yourself as you read the words "God keeps Satan on a leash." The images they conjure up in your mind must be comical, to say the least. I wish I had the gift of being able to draw, because you'd find a graphic with a calm, cool, collected God holding on to a desperate Satan by a leash, using just a single finger. That would be quite a picture.

Now, how about this picture—a preacher in the midst of a rousing exhortation on the battle between good and evil. Imagine the preacher getting really worked up as he or she warns their congregation that they must choose up sides because the battle is going right down to the wire. Well, unfortunately, the latter is easy to picture. "Fury of hell" sermons about the battle between good and evil, or God and Satan, are commonplace. It hardly matters what denomination. I've actually known people to leave a church service more depressed than when they went in because the preacher scared them into believing Satan might be winning. This is pure, unadulterated bondage. Satan may appear to be having a field day on earth these days, but that's only because God is allowing it.

Just Who's in Charge?

In 2 Corinthians 4:4, we learn that Satan is the "god of this age." At this time in history, during this age, Satan rules. This is his realm. We, as believers, are aliens in a foreign environment. To further illustrate this fact, turn to Ephesians 2:2. Here Paul calls Satan "the prince of the power of the air, the spirit who now works in the sons of disobedience."

There's no doubt Satan has power, but let's make no mistake about who is in charge. Satan has power only because God is allowing it. Satan has no power other than that which is permitted him by God. We know this through the story of Job. The first chapter of the book of Job is an excellent portrayal of the truth that Satan's power is limited. Let's look at verses 6-12:

> Now there was a day when the sons of God came to present themselves before the Lord, and Satan also came among them. And the Lord said to Satan, "From where do you come?"
>
> So Satan answered the Lord and said, "From going to and fro on the earth and from walking back and forth on it."
>
> Then the Lord said to Satan, "Have you considered My servant Job, that there is none like him on the earth, a blameless and upright man, one who fears God and shuns evil?"

> *So Satan answered the* Lord *and said, "Does Job fear God for nothing? Have You not made a hedge around him, around his household, and around all that he has on every side? You have blessed the work of his hands, and his possessions have increased in the land. But now, stretch out Your hand and touch all that he has, and he will surely curse You to Your face!"*
>
> *And the* Lord *said to Satan, "Behold, all that he has is in your power; only do not lay a hand on his person."*
>
> *So Satan went out from the presence of the* Lord.

There are a few truths in those verses to note. First, Satan is actively roaming the face of the earth. He's going back and forth looking for opportunities to wreak havoc. But the more important truth is that Satan's power is limited in reach, scope, and time. Notice he didn't even consider doing anything to Job until after God had suggested it to him. Job feared God and thus was an alien on the earth. He didn't belong to Satan. He belonged to God—and Satan's authority stops at the doorstep of the believer. Satan cannot harm someone that belongs to God without God's permission. We see this truth again in Luke 22:31, when Jesus lets Peter know that Satan had come asking permission to harm him. Jesus apparently gave permission to Satan to test Peter, yet He told Peter that He had prayed that his faith would not fail. This promise must certainly have been Peter's only comfort when he realized he had denied the Lord three times.

Satan's Days Are Numbered

Going back to Job, we also note that God defined parameters for Satan. He could torment Job and cause him much stress and anxiety, but Satan was not allowed to harm him physically—to "lay a hand on his person." This was God's decree, and Satan had to honor it. Do you think for one minute that if Satan and God were of equal power that Satan would have followed God's command?

In Job 2:6, God again says to Satan, "Behold, he is in your hand, but spare his life." I would bet that if Satan had had any power to disobey this direct command from God, he would have done so in a skinny minute. This was a golden opportunity to show God who was boss. But we know what happened. Satan did indeed cause tremendous disaster in Job's life, but that was it. Job lived to be 140 years old, and God restored all that Satan had taken away and then some. Job 42:12 reports that the "Lord blessed the latter days of Job more than his beginning." Satan has power—but only that which God allows.

In fact, even Satan's days are numbered by God. We already know Satan's ultimate fate. Jesus clues us in: "Now is the judgment of this world; now the ruler of this world will be cast out" (John 12:31). There's no contest between God and Satan; that's already been decided. The book of Revelation tells us what is going to happen. God's work is finished[26]—and the end has already been determined. God wins. Satan loses.

To say that God is dueling Satan for power is giving way too much power to Satan—not to mention it's biblically inaccurate. God is not battling Satan anymore than a three-year-old child battles their parent. The parent may allow the child some privileges and will even let the child throw a temper tantrum every now and then, but the parent is in charge. Despite the fact the child may think they are in control, they are not. The parent controls the child's destiny. In the world of the parent–child relationship, the parent is sovereign. In our world, both seen and unseen, God is sovereign. He may have allowed certain powers to Satan, but He remains in complete control.

Satan Didn't Catch God by Surprise

Then, of course, there is the question of where Satan came from. Did he just pop up from out of nowhere to be a thorn in God's side? To answer that we have to go way back to the beginning, even before Genesis 1:1. Satan was a created being—when exactly created, we do not know, but it was certainly before he showed up in the Garden of Eden. Herein is another argument for Satan not being equal to God. The thing that is created is never equal or superior to its creator.

In Ezekiel 28:14, we learn that he was an "anointed cherub." The Hebrew translation of *anointed* is "appointed to a special place and function." The exact reason Satan was created is not fully known, but we do know it was for God's divine purpose, because God works everything according to His purpose.[27] We know Satan rebelled against God and was cast out of heaven, along with a host of his angels. Satan then showed up to deceive Adam and Eve.

But none of this caught God by surprise. God knew exactly what Satan would do and had an answer planned long before Satan had the idea. Revelation 13:8 mentions what I believe is the most powerful and reassuring phrase of the entire Bible—the "Lamb slain from the foundation of the world." Wow! God had a leash on Satan from the very beginning. In other words, if God hadn't known and planned for Satan's antics, why did He plan His redemption process in Jesus? God knew, God ordained, and God had Jesus in mind before He ever created Satan. God created Satan, just as He has all of us, for His purpose. Satan is playing out the hand and role that God has given Him, but no more and no less. God's plan is perfect, even though Satan is not.

We don't know, and certainly can't and won't understand, *why* God created Satan in the first place. That is a question theologians have been debating for centuries. However, we do know there's a purpose for everything, even though we don't always know what that purpose is. Just as God planned the redemption process through Jesus, He also planned the "fall of man."

You Need to Have the Right Fixation

Here is where Satan comes in. He is the father of lies. He was a "liar and murderer from the beginning" (John 8:44). One of Satan's principal aims is to get us to doubt God, the exact opposite of trusting. The world makes us feel sometimes that God is not enough. Have you ever heard the popular expression, "If it is to be, it's up to me"? Satan doesn't want people to trust God. He wants people to believe the lie that human beings are in control of their destiny. The more we feel in control, the less dependence we'll have on God. This is the exact lie he told Adam and Eve in the Garden. Satan told them that they could "be like God" (Genesis 3:5).

Unfortunately, many still buy into this lie to this very day. There are even some religions that teach the concept that human beings are all gods, that we control our own destiny. This teaching is false, and therefore can lead only to frustration and anxiety. Peace can only be accomplished by relinquishing our attempts to be in control. Jesus spoke in John 14:27 of true peace—and it isn't achieved through the world. In fact, when we experience anxiety, worry, depression, anger, and frustration, it is a result of viewing our current circumstances from the worldly perspective. We are measuring our life experience by the world's definition of an ideal and satisfying life.

And nowhere did God promise us that our life on earth would be all fun and roses. Just the opposite is true. Jesus proclaims in John 16:33,

> *These things I have spoken to you, that in Me you may have peace. In the world you will have tribulation; but be of good cheer, I have overcome the world.*

The bottom line is that we can expect trials, tribulations, disappointments, and challenges because we are in enemy territory.

But the war is already won. We can rest in the fact that the Lord is working His life through us in preparation for the "next world." When we give up our own power, we can then begin to fully experience His power. Our peace, while on this planet, is attainable only by viewing our life as belonging to God. Thus we should always be looking above for our strength. Paul writes in Colossians 3:2, "Set your mind on things above." The Greek word for "set" in that passage means to have a "fixation." Just glancing above every now and then is not enough. We need to have a fixation on God. This means giving up ourselves and not focusing on what we see in the world, but we know to be true in God. There's no ultimate power in Satan. There's no independent power in the world. There's no power in and of ourselves. The only sovereign power comes from God.[28]

You Need Help—and God Offers More Than You've Ever Dreamed

If we should expect tribulations and, in them, look to God for our peace, what kinds of help can we expect from God? Can we or should we look to Him for any help? The answer is *yes*. We shouldn't fear Satan because God is always at work in the lives of believers. Sometimes He takes us down the path of trials and difficulties, and other times the path of great prosperity, but He's always on the throne and always in charge. His plan is not always understandable or even recognizable to us, but He's always present in our lives.[29]

The problem is that God's help doesn't always match our worldly expectations or limited perspective. From our earthly view, things are often a mess and out of control, but from God's view, all is exactly in place and going as He decreed—even if we don't get it.

I love Isaiah 40:31 because it gives us an insight into the kinds of help we can expect from God. It's a famous verse, one that I'll bet you've seen on plaques or posters:

Those who wait on the Lord shall renew their strength; they shall mount up with wings like eagles, they shall run and not be weary, they shall walk and not faint.

That sounds inspiring, but look closer. The three images Isaiah uses parallel the kinds of help we can and should expect from our everpresent Commander In Chief. (In fact, the Hebrew word for *wait* used in this passage means *to expect*.[30])

When He Changes Things

The first kind of help is the kind we all want. We want to mount up with wings like eagles. This is the kind of help we ask for in prayer. We pray that God would miraculously change our circumstances. We pray that He would reach down in His infinite sovereignty and fix whatever needs fixing. To us, it seems like the best possible kind of help. We ask and He transforms.

I ask for this kind of help all the time. I've prayed countless times for those I know who are suffering with health issues to be miraculously healed, members of my own family included. As a professional speaker, I can recall many times begging God to suddenly swoop down like a divine eagle and drop business on my doorstep. Sometimes He did—but more often than not, God chose not to transform my circumstances. He chose another way of helping.

When He Empowers Us to Change Things

Many times, God empowers me to transform my own circumstances. This way of helping is to "run and not grow weary." God simply gives us the strength to keep on keeping on, to run and finish what we started. (This way is not our preference. It's easier to have God swoop in and transform our tribulations into triumphs.) However, when God chooses to empower us, it is absolutely critical to remember who is supplying the power. It's easy to think it was of your own doing. This is one of Satan's worldly traps.

Paul talks about pride and false humility in Colossians chapter 2. In context, he's writing about what happens when we try to win favor with God by following special religious practices. But the same wrong attitudes come when we get full of ourselves over what we achieve, even

> A car has no power without fuel. It may look pretty and have all the nicest features, but it still won't travel a single foot until the energy to make it run is supplied. You are like a car. You will not run a single mile without the energy of God.

though it's through divine empowerment. "Vainly puffed up his fleshly mind" is the way Paul puts it in verse 18. Later, in verses 20-23, he writes,

> If you died with Christ from the basic principles of the world, why, as though living in the world, do you subject yourselves to regulations—[such as] do not touch, do not taste, do not handle, which all concern things which perish with the using—according to the commandments and doctrines of men? These things indeed have an appearance of wisdom in self-imposed religion, false humility, and neglect of the body, but are of no value against the indulgences of the flesh.

To put it another way, you are never going to be perfect on your own. So when you do something right, don't be so foolish as to think it was of your own doing. You are not even of this world, so why take credit for things you do in this world? Your strength is from above. Your reward is from above as well. God chooses to empower you—you are only the vessel. A car has no power without fuel. It may look pretty and have all the nicest features, but it still won't travel a single foot until the energy to make it run is supplied. You are like a car. You will not run a single mile without the energy of God.

When Things Don't Change

Isaiah's picture of walking and not fainting describes the third and final way God chooses to help. This is where God doesn't transform our circumstances, nor does He give *us* the power to transform our circumstances. He simply sustains us so we can endure the circumstances. (That was what He did with Job.) This, of course, is not what we would choose at all. This kind of help is not fun. Things may not change. Things may not get better. We take our lumps and keep going.

One of the biggest myths of the Bible is that God will not give you a problem greater than you can bear. The passage most people point to is 1 Corinthians 10:13, which promises that God "will not allow you to be tempted beyond what you are able, but with the temptation will also make the way of escape, that you may be able to bear it." In context, it's clear that Paul is talking about temptation to *sin,* not the tempting (testing) involved in everyday struggles and difficult circumstances.

No, the apostle was not talking about enduring hardships. You may be faced with earthly challenges that will overwhelm you. The Bible is full of examples of believers who underwent pain and suffering that was beyond the limits of human endurance. In 2 Corinthians 1:8, Paul himself wrote of being "burdened beyond measure, above strength, so that we despaired even of life." He was writing about circumstances so hard he even feared for his life. In verse 9, he continued, "Yes, we had the sentence of death in ourselves, that we should not trust in ourselves but in God who raises the dead." Paul endured by not trusting in this world or in his own strength but by trusting in God. That was the only way he was able to endure. That was the only way he was able to walk and not faint, even when he was being attacked by Satan.

We often make the mistake of believing that when we battle hardship and things don't get any better (in fact, they may be getting worse), God is simply not present or is unwilling to help. His help just may not match our request, though. He may be just sustaining us as we live through our tough circumstances.

Help Comes According to His Plan

We've all heard the famous poem about footprints in the sand. The writer wrote of seeing two sets of footprints in the sand, one his, the other God's. There were two sets for every occasion in his life—except during the extremely hard times there was only one set. He questioned God, and God replied, "It was then I carried you in my arms."

Now, I know I paraphrased and shortened that story tremendously, but it's a wonderful example of God's "ever-presence" in our lives. Sometimes He carries us on wings like eagles and changes our circumstances. Sometimes He empowers us to run and not grow weary, thus allowing us to change our circumstances. Yet sometimes He just allows us not to faint. Circumstances don't change, and we must endure, even when Satan may be pummeling our life.[31]

Nevertheless, God is sovereign over all the circumstances of our life—good, bad, and everything in between—and *any* power granted to Satan is ultimately designed to accomplish the Lord's purposes. Surely the cross and the resurrection are the greatest picture of this reality. Satan brought sin into the human race, and this brought death. Yet the Lord demonstrated His glory and His power through conquering both sin and death!

⁓∾

The bottom line is, Satan has no power over the life of the believer that has not been permitted him from above. Jesus said this very thing in John 19:11 when He answered the Roman governor Pilate: "You could have no power at all against Me unless it had been given you from above." Jesus knew it wasn't

Pilate, or Satan, or fate, or any other man that was in control—but God, and God alone.

Sure, we don't have the benefit of the big picture. We're just ground troops in enemy territory. One of the great passages that helps us in our limited perspectives is Joseph's words in Genesis 50:20:

You meant evil against me; but God meant it for good, in order to bring about as it is this day, to save many people alive.

Tragedies happen, and often we immediately think evil is winning. And according to the world, it may be. But we are not of this world.[32] We belong to God. And fear not—He has Satan on a very short leash!

Part Two
Moving Forward with the Truths

9

Why Are These Truths So Important?

A few years ago, when I spoke at a Christian conference in Denver, a fellow speaker on the program challenged me with a very pertinent question. He asked me, "Why argue about the minor points of theology? Why not just major in the majors, and minor in the minors?"

I didn't have a very good answer—I guess because I had never thought of these truths as minor. The very notion that these truths were insignificant when compared to the "bigger" truths had never occurred to me. I guess if I had to take a stab on what might be considered a "major" truth, it would John 3:16. Jesus is the risen Son of God, and anyone who believes in Him will have eternal life. That is big stuff. But outside of that, what makes one truth major and another truth minor?

It was a good question. It made me think long and hard, and I have come to an important conclusion. There's no such thing as major or minor. All truth is important—and understanding one point, as minor as it may appear, has bearing on the understanding of another. Even the truth of John 3:16 is better understood and appreciated in light of its nuances and implications. Further, nowhere in the Bible is it even remotely suggested that some truths are greater than others. The entire Bible is entirely major. In this chapter, I will attempt to pinpoint why each truth is important and focus on the net effect each has on the life of the believer.

Why Doesn't God Grade on a Curve?

No one truth is more important than another, but there does seem to be an order in which each truth hinges on the understanding of the preceding one. The first truth—that God doesn't grade on a curve—seems logically first because it is crucial for us to realize God demands perfection. One of my favorite seminar questions is a true-or-false one, and I'll ask it of you. Only perfect people go to heaven—true or false? The answer, of course, is *true*. Only perfect people do go to heaven, but the "perfect" that is required is not worldly perfection, but perfect in God's eyes.

That kind of perfect is far more specific and stringent than any definition of perfect that might be acceptable to the world. God requires us to be perfect in thought, word, and deed. This is not just perfection in what we say, or even what we do, but in what we don't say and what we don't do. Perfection is required inside and out.

This is a pivotal truth. My sister once told me of a comment made from a friend of our family that illustrates its importance. Our friend remarked that she believed she sometimes goes days at a time without committing a single sin. In essence, she is able to achieve perfection for several days in a row. I wonder if she has ever resorted to keeping score. I mean, what's the record? How many days is she able to go before she sins? What is her goal? More importantly, who is she trying to fool? There may be some people who actually believe she is able to be perfect...but does she really believe it herself?

God doesn't cut anyone any slack. We must be perfect. The good news is that there is a way to achieve the kind of perfection God requires—by believing in Jesus. A good Bible passage to keep reminding yourself of is John 6:28-29. Jesus was asked point-blank, "What shall we do, that we may work the works of God?" In other words, how can we be perfect in God's eyes? Jesus answered, "This is the work of God, that you believe in Him whom He sent." Jesus could have gone on about all the things we needed to do to gain God's acceptance. He had the opportunity. However, His answer was clear. Believe in Me. There is only one way to be perfect, and that is by believing in Jesus. Jesus was perfect, and if we believe in Him, His righteousness is extended to us (Romans 4:5).

Bottom line, this truth should make us humble. Knowing that God requires perfection and that we can't do it on our own—only through Jesus—should cause us to fall flat on our face in humility. This is a good thing. Once we recognize our own imperfections, we can be more compassionate toward others and humble. Jesus commanded us in Matthew 7:1 to "judge not, that you be not judged." The psalmist wrote in Psalm 130:3, "If You, Lord, should mark iniquities, O Lord, who could stand?" The answer is, *no one*. By realizing it is only by the perfection of Christ we may satisfy

God, we become humble and bow to the One through whom we *can* become perfect.

If you're so led, pray this little prayer with me:

Dear Father, I realize You require perfection, and this is not something I am able to achieve on my own. I am most humble and grateful today that You have provided a way to achieve perfection in Your eyes—and that is through Your Son, Jesus, who is the perfect gift for imperfect people. It is through Jesus we have our hope. It is through Jesus You show Your ultimate love. I am humbled. Amen.

Why Can't Dead People Help Themselves?

This leads us directly to the second truth of this book—dead people can't help themselves. God requires perfection, but the real problem is we are born imperfect. Imperfect people can never be perfect. Sure, there are certain things we can change. We can change hair colors. We can change the shape of our bodies. We can change addresses and change friends, but there are a few things we can't change. You can't change your mother and father, and you can't change the fact that we are all born spiritually dead and imperfect.

The Bible puts it this way: "Can the Ethiopian change his skin or the leopard its spots?"[33] The obvious answer is *no*. Those are among the things we can't change. And we can't change the condition in which we are born. In Psalm 51:5, David writes, "I was brought forth in iniquity, and in sin my mother conceived me." We are born physically alive but spiritually dead. We need to be born again, but this is not something we can do on our own. A dead person can't do much to help himself. We need to be made alive spiritually to be able to accept Jesus by faith. This is not something we can do alone. We must have help from above.

In 1 Corinthians 12:3 we read, "No one can say that Jesus is Lord except by the Holy Spirit." This is a gift of God. We need to be born again by the Spirit before we ever call on Jesus. It's not about us. It's called *grace.* "By grace you have been saved through faith, and that not of yourselves; it is a gift of God, not of works, lest anyone should boast" (Ephesians 2:8-9). Grace is unmerited favor. We don't deserve to be given new life, but it is a gift, the ultimate gift from God. And it isn't because of anything we did. That's why grace is a free gift. There are no strings attached.

Some gifts come with strings attached, both spoken and unspoken. This is not the case with grace. We were dead in our physical lineage in Adam, but we're alive in our spiritual lineage in Christ. In Romans 5:17, Paul writes,

> *If by the one man's offense death reigned through the one, much more those who receive abundance of grace and of the gift of righteousness will reign in life through the One, Jesus Christ.*

Notice the word *one* was not capitalized when talking about Adam, but it was when referring to Jesus. Jesus is the One through whom we are saved by grace. It's God's gift.

I don't know about you, but the net effect of this truth on me is pure and simple thankfulness. Whenever I think of this gift, I can't help but close my eyes and say "thank You" over and over again. Martin Luther once said, "The fewer the words, the better the prayer." I often am reminded of that saying when all I say in a prayer is "thank You." That says it all. Pray with me if you feel that way too.

Most gracious Father, no words can ever express how thankful I

*am for the gift of faith. It is by Your grace I am saved. I recognize
I didn't deserve Your grace, nor did I do anything to merit it. I
fully accept it as a gift. I know I don't say it enough, but thank
You. I am alive because of You, and it is through Your Son I pray
today. Amen.*

Why Were the Ten Commandments Not Given to Be Kept?

The third truth is an extension of the first two truths. If
the perfection is gained only through belief in Jesus, and even
that belief is an unearned, unmerited gift from God, the Ten
Commandments—let alone the entire law—cannot be the path
to righteousness. In fact, Paul calls the law "the ministry of death,
written and engraved on stones."[34] God's first law to man was not
to eat the fruit of the tree of the knowledge of good and evil, but it
was broken. That led to the fall of man. If man couldn't keep the
first law, what makes us think we can keep God's other laws?

The truth is, we can't keep them, nor did God ultimately intend
for us to. The purpose of the law was to make us understand our
need for a Savior and point us to Christ. As we saw in Galatians
3:24, "The law was our tutor to bring us to Christ," and in verse 25,
"But after faith has come, we are no longer under a tutor." Once we
become born again and believe in Jesus, the Ten Commandments
and the law have done their job. That isn't to say that they aren't
good rules to live by while you're on this earth. They are still
useful as good rules of conduct, but their intended purpose has
been fulfilled.

Believers now live by a new law that is "written in their hearts"
(Romans 2:15), and that is the "law of faith" (Romans 3:27). Any
attempt to be justified by trying to keep the law is a slap in God's
face. Paul writes in Galatians 5:4, "You have become estranged

from Christ, you who attempt to be justified by law; you have fallen from grace." God wants us to live by grace, not by the law. In verse 18 of the same chapter of Galatians, Paul writes, "If you are led by the Spirit, you are not under the law." Faith in Jesus, which is a free

For believers, the law has done its job. What God now wants is surrender... God wants us to wave the white flag.

gift from God, has fulfilled the requirements of the law and made us perfect in God's eyes. That statement capsules the first three truths of this book into one sentence. For believers, the law has done its job.

What God now wants is surrender—that should be the net effect of this truth. God wants us to wave the white flag. But exactly how do you surrender? I believe it is a matter of giving up control. Human beings want control. We want to control everything, including salvation. A pastor at a prominent church in my area was quoted as saying during one of his sermons, "If I were God, I'd make it so that tithing was the litmus test for going to heaven." Sounds so easy, and so controllable. Just do this and you'll go to heaven. (Besides, tithing would also be a good thing for the church's checkbook!) But he isn't God, and isn't in control.

God wants us to be out of control. He wants us to realize that apart from Him, we cannot do anything that is good. The prophet Isaiah put it this way: "All our righteousnesses are like filthy rags."[35] The key word is *our*. Any of *our* works are like filthy rags. If any commandment or law were used as a litmus test, then we'd live in constant judgment and fear. *Did I give enough? Was I kind enough? Was my neighbor courteous enough? Is my wife faithful enough? Are my kids respectful enough?* Tithing should not be a litmus test, nor should being "good," nor should observing the law or the Ten Commandments. The only litmus test is Jesus.

Thus there's no need to fear God's judgment, nor should we judge others. Whenever you need a gentle reminder of this truth, read and reread the book of Galatians. Paul writes in it,

> *I do not set aside the grace of God; for if righteousness comes through the law, then Christ died in vain (2:21).*

That's a powerful truth to understand. The more quickly and deeply we understand that truth, the more we will naturally surrender to His power. And there's no power in the law—in fact, sin gets its strength through the law (1 Corinthians 15:56). The only power is Christ Himself.

I often ask God to help me surrender. My prayer goes like this:

> *Dear God, I know that apart from Jesus I can do no good in Your eyes. The purpose of Your law was to drive us to the end of ourselves and get us to surrender to Your Son. It is only through Jesus that Your commands are fulfilled—and the work of the cross is complete and sufficient. I bow down before You today and ask for Your help in surrendering. I don't want to judge nor be judged by any other human. The only judge I need is Your Spirit. I surrender to You. Amen.*

Why Is What You See in the Mirror Not the Real You?

If we dwell on what we see, we will never find rest and security. A few of my closest friends have confided in me that they avoid the mirror at all costs. They don't like what they see. They tell me it just depresses them to see all their flaws, wrinkles, and flabbiness. It's much easier to not look.

The good news, though, is what we see is not who we are. We are not the outside, but rather the inside. The outside may look bleak, but the inside has never looked better. We read this very truth in 2 Corinthians 4:16:

We do not lose heart. Even though our outward man is perishing, yet the inward man is being renewed day by day.

Verses 17 and 18 are just as powerful. Verse 18 says, "We do not look at the things which are seen, but at the things which are not seen. For the things which are seen are temporary, but the things which are not seen are eternal." The outside is temporary. The inside is eternal. Jesus said that whoever believes in Him shall have eternal life. Therefore, *we* are the internal, not the external.

Turn to Romans 8:9-10 for further understanding: "You are not in the flesh, but in the Spirit." In verse 10 Paul continues, "And if Christ is in you, the body is dead because of sin, but the Spirit is life because of righteousness." We are a new creation in Christ, and that means we are perfect. If Christ is in us, it doesn't get any better than that. It's a matter of understanding your identity in Christ.

And the fruit of this understanding is security. If we are "in Christ," then we have security. It's that simple. Just bookmark 2 Corinthians 1:21-22 as the place to go whenever you start to question your eternal security:

He who establishes us with you in Christ and has anointed us is God, who also has sealed us and given us the Spirit in our hearts as a guarantee.

Our identity is God's guarantee! That's the purpose of the Spirit, to seal us in Christ and keep us blameless until we stand in the presence of God.[36] It's not something we need to worry about— the Spirit will see to it.

I can't speak for you, but upon learning this truth, I breathed a huge sigh of relief. If we still believe that what we see in the mirror is our real identity, then we are dooming ourselves to a life of constant worry. There's no security in what we see, only through what we don't see. It's the life of faith. It's easy to believe in something we see; that doesn't require any faith. Faith is believing in things we don't see. It's believing the Word, instead of our eyes. It's knowing who we are in Christ.*

If you're led, pray with me:

> *Dear Lord, I am reminded every day when I look into the mirror of my imperfections. Before, this used to get me down, but now I know that what I see is not the real me. It's not what You see. I still see the old man, but You see the new man. You don't even see the sins of the old man any longer.*[37] *You see the light of Your Spirit. You see the light of Christ. I can be secure knowing that Your Spirit was given to me as a guarantee. I can be secure knowing I belong to You. I can be secure knowing my identity is You. Amen.*

Why Will Trying to Live for Jesus Only Frustrate You?

If it's not us who lives, but Christ who lives in us, then doesn't it make sense that it's fruitless to live for Jesus, and rather just rejoice in Jesus living through us?

Many Christians readily embrace the truth that what we see in the mirror isn't the person that God sees, but then they embark on a life of trying to polish up the fleshly image. Flesh can never get "cleaned up" enough to satisfy God. A life that stems from the performance of the flesh will not only be frustrating, but it will never please God. Never, ever. When we as believers resort to

---

* Steve McVey, who wrote the foreword to this book, is a master at teaching this truth. I would highly recommend you buy one of his books—*Grace Walk*, *Grace Rules*, or *Grace Amazing*—for further understanding of who you are.

trying to live according to the flesh, we are denying our identity and setting ourselves up for despair.

In Romans 8:5, Paul writes,

Those who live according to the flesh set their minds on the things of the flesh, but those who live according to the Spirit, the things of the Spirit.

But then catch verse 6: "To be carnally minded is death, but to be spiritually minded is life and peace." The fruit of understanding this truth is peace. It's one thing to know intellectually that the real "you" is the life of Christ that resides inside; it's another ball game to live your life that way. But that's what Paul is talking about. Live your life according to your real identity and not by the flesh you see in the mirror. If you do that, you will find peace.

The opposite is living by the flesh—a never-ending commitment to trying to please God. It's a constant cycle of condemnation and rededication. It works like this: When you focus on the dying outer flesh, you are continually being reminded of all that is wrong in your life. You feel condemned and repeatedly ask God for forgiveness and rededicate your life to Jesus.

That may sound good, but there are several problems with it. First, there is *no* condemnation for those who are in Christ, which we saw previously in Romans 8:1. It makes sense. How could there be any condemnation if Jesus, the Son of God, is living inside you and is now your true identity?

Second, it's unnecessary to continually ask God for forgiveness. You've been forgiven once and for all. The work of the cross is sufficient for the sins of your flesh—all of them—the past, present, and future sins. Think about it. When Jesus died on the cross, you were not yet a physical being. All of your sins were at that time future sins. He didn't just die on the cross at the moment you became a believer. That moment marks the occasion you began to belong to Christ and should be celebrated, but that happened in God's eyes a long time ago. In John 1:12-13 we read,

> As many as received Him, to them He gave the right to become children of God, to those who believe in His name: who were born, not of blood, nor of the will of the flesh, nor of the will of man, but of God.

You were a child of God's long before you were a child of your mother and father.

Lastly, there's no need to rededicate yourself to God. You may want to do it as a public expression of your faith, but do it as a celebration, not as a gesture to "try" to do better. Living by the Spirit means to understand you already are a child of God. And there's no need to "try" to do any better than that! God will never love you any more than He already does! We're either trying or trusting—and God prefers we trust in Him and allow Jesus to live through us. It's a peace issue—the peace that surpasses all understanding.[38] Pray with me:

> Dear heavenly Father, from this day forward I live by my true identity. I give up trying to do better, and I put that in Your capable hands. Psalm 57:2 tells us it's You "who performs all things for me." In 1 Thessalonians 5:24, Your word again tells us "He who calls you is faithful, who also will do it." My job is to trust. My job is to find peace and rest in You. It's my inheritance—and I thank You for it. Amen.

Why Doesn't Prayer Change God's Mind?

Prayer is a big part of the life of a believer, and it's ordained by God as a means of communication with Him. Prayer must be instrumental somehow in God's plan. Well, it is. Prayer is one of the means God uses to accomplish His plan, but it never changes His plan. The very picture of God saying, "Okay, you win—I'll do it your way instead," is an abomination to the truth of a sovereign God. Either God is sovereign or prayer is sovereign. It can't be both. God uses prayer, and sometimes He even grants the requests in our prayers, but it was because that's what He had already intended to do. Prayer afforded us the privilege of being part of the action. Prayer is a lifeline to God, and it's through prayer we find out what He's doing in our life. Prayer is an ordained means of finding contentment, not finding restlessness.

However, restlessness is exactly what we'll find if we believe we can affect God's plan. There could never be any rest in that. If prayer were sovereign and could change God's plan, we'd never be content with our circumstances because we'd forever be pleading our case for things to be the way we think they should be. I am a middle-aged guy, and if there's one thing I know now that I didn't know when I was younger, it's that I rarely know what is best for my life. Things I thought I wanted ended up to be fool's gold, and things I never would have known to ask for turned out to be exactly what I needed.

In other words, we are incapable of knowing what we need. We don't have the luxury of the big picture. Even times I've thought were good times at the moment turned out, in hindsight, to be not that great—and vice versa. I am thankful that God is sovereign and it is His plan that will prevail, not mine. What this does is produce contentment. I can be content with my life, just as things are, because I know things are exactly as God would have them be.

Of course, I continue to pray for things that seem right at the time, but I am sure to begin every request with "If it be Your will," and end every request with "Not my will, but Your will be done."

This is exactly how Jesus taught us how to pray. Some of the most important words of the Lord's Prayer are, "Thy will be done, on earth as it is in heaven."

The ultimate image of this kind of contentment is from the book of Daniel. Remember the story of Shadrach, Meshach, and Abednego? King Nebuchadnezzar was going to cast them into a fiery furnace if they didn't bow down and worship the idols he had set up. Catch their answer in Daniel 3:1-18:

> *If that is the case, our God whom we serve is able to deliver us from the burning fiery furnace, and He will deliver us from your hand, O king. But if not, let it be known to you, O king, that we do not serve your gods, nor will we worship the gold image which you have set up.*

They believed God would save them—and I'm sure they prayed to that effect—but they were also willing to accept that it might not be in God's plan and were at peace.

We can indeed be content, but only after we acknowledge He alone is sovereign and His will will be done. I find contentment in Isaiah 46:10 particularly, which speaks of God "declaring the end from the beginning, and from ancient times things that are not yet done, saying 'My counsel shall stand, and I will do all My pleasure.'" It is His good pleasure that will be done. It is for us to accept and find contentment in the fact that He knows what is best for us. Let's pray for contentment:

> *Dear God, I come before You today humbly acknowledging Your omnipotence. I often think I know what's best for my life. When my requests match Your answer, I think You've answered me directly, but when Your answer doesn't match my request, I feel abandoned. This is because I expect certain things and want to*

*be in control, rather than be content in the glory of Your will.
Teach me to pray the way Your Son taught the world to pray and
to be content in whatever You may bring to pass. If it be Your
will, protect me from harm, but if not, let me find contentment.
For Your will alone shall be done. Amen.*

How Does It Help Us to Understand That God Keeps Satan on a Leash?

As Christians, we shouldn't live in fear, but rather in the
comfort of knowing that we are in God's hands and that no one
can change that.[39] Not even Satan.

The net effect of understanding this truth is love—pure and
simple love. No other truth illuminates God's love like realizing
He has complete control of everything. Let's look at a few passages
from Scripture that support this truth. How about this one from
Colossians 1:16:

*By Him all things were created that are in heaven and that are
on earth, visible and invisible, whether thrones or dominions or
principalities or powers. All things were created through Him
and for Him.*

Notice it said *all* things. Not just some things, or good things,
but *all* things. Need another? Look at Hebrews 2:8: "He put all in
subjection under him. He left nothing that is not put under him."
This includes Satan.

Satan doesn't operate outside of God's sovereignty. Satan may
think he's in control, but ultimately he is not. He cannot harm a
believer unless God has given him permission to do so.

The bottom line is love. You are set aside for God's purpose.
That doesn't mean your life will be all roses and sunshine. You

will have setbacks and heartaches. Nowhere in the Bible does God promise every believer a life without hardship. You will have pain—but God is always in control.

I've heard, and suspect you have too, that God is in the big things. He doesn't have time to worry about the minute details of everyone's life. He's got bigger fish to fry. To believe this means that some things Satan does might slip under God's radar—that the world is simply too big for God to be in all places at all times. That may be a natural, human way of thinking, but it's simply not true. God is a God of details. He is in everything.

> **I remember planning and doing everything for my children when they were incapable of doing it for themselves...I didn't do it to exercise my authority, but because I loved them. It's that simple—and it's that way with God.**

Consider the teachings of Jesus in Matthew 10:29-31. This is Jesus speaking:

Are not two sparrows sold for a copper coin? And not one of them falls to the ground apart from your Father's will. But the very hairs of your head are all numbered. Do not fear therefore; you are of more value than many sparrows.

These few short sentences tell us a lot. First, it tells us that God is in the details. He is responsible for sparrows falling to the ground and the very hairs of our head. Second, it tells us that God has those activities planned. They were in the Father's will, which means they were predestined.

Lastly, the passage tells us that God loves us immeasurably. For God to have planned our every step and minor detail shows He cares about us. If God didn't care, He would turn His back, and certainly wouldn't waste time on things that aren't important.

We are important to God. He loves His children, and therefore He leaves nothing to chance. I remember planning and doing everything for my children when they were incapable of doing it for themselves. I brushed their teeth, spoon-fed them, held the tissue to blow their nose, and just about anything else you can think of. I didn't do it to exercise my authority, but because I loved them. It's that simple—and it's that way with God.

God has a plan for my life and your life. Nothing will stand in the way of that plan. Not the elements of nature, not strangers on the street, not bad luck, and not Satan. God keeps Satan on a leash and that truth is an ultimate expression of God's love. Here is one final prayer:

Dear Father God, words cannot express how thankful and peaceful I feel that You, and You alone, are in ultimate control of everything that happens. Many times I don't understand the things that happen, but I trust Your Word, which says that all things work together for Your glory. I am thankful and peaceful that You know and have planned for everything, down to the hair on my head. That shows Your love, and it shows Your sovereignty. Times may be troubled, but You are always on Your throne and in control. "Yea, though I walk through the valley of the shadow of death, I will fear no evil; for You are with me; Your rod and Your staff, they comfort me."[40] Amen.

10 Sharing These Truths with Others

I've gotten a wide array of reactions through the years as I've attempted to share the truths in this book with others. Naturally, some of them are easier for some people to believe than for other people, but the reactions basically fall into two categories.

First, there are those who dismiss them outright. They know what they believe—and this isn't it. Some dismiss these truths because they simply interpret the Bible differently. Although I believe the Bible is as clear as a bright, sunny day, I must confess that theologians have debated some of the truths discussed in this book for centuries. I do not attempt to change anyone's mind. If the apostle Paul, Martin Luther, John Calvin, Jonathan Edwards, and Charles Spurgeon weren't able to convince the biblical scholars of their time, David Rich certainly will not either.

But then there are those who are not knowledgeable theologians but simply have a different interpretation. They just do not believe these truths because they sound foreign to them. They haven't heard them preached in their churches, or they don't match their self-conceived image of God. I've run into scores of people who find comfort in believing they can manipulate God by praying "hard" enough. There are also some people who believe they came to accept Christ because they were smart enough to accept the truth when they heard it. Some simply believe in the sovereignty of the "free will" of man rather than the "free grace" of a sovereign God. Pride is one of the biggest barriers to enjoying the fruits of the truth.

Regardless, however, of the reasons why some don't believe these truths, it is usually not beneficial to debate. There are just some issues believers will not see eye-to-eye on this side of heaven. That's okay with me. It's not my place to convince, nor is it my place to judge. I didn't write this book for those who know what they believe and are comfortable with it. I don't want this book to be used as a dividing line. I simply want to shed light on truths that rarely get explored.

Who I Wrote This Book For

Rather, I wrote this book for people in the second category I mentioned—those who aren't sure what they believe, or at least are open to further understanding. It's that group of people with whom I feel most compelled to share these truths.

That was the case with me. I felt pretty certain I knew what I believed. After all, I had gone to church my entire life and was even a choirboy when I was a child. I'd listened to thousands of sermons. So when I was confronted with these truths, my first reaction was not to believe. But something at least led me to head straight to the Word for clarification. (Perhaps it was nothing more than arrogant pride. I wanted to prove my teacher wrong.)

However, the more I searched to debunk what I had heard, the more I became convinced of the truth. I couldn't understand why I hadn't heard of these truths sooner. It transformed everything. I felt closer to the Lord, more secure in my inheritance, and more humble. Grace took on an even heightened meaning. I had sung "Amazing Grace" dozens of times in my life, but now I can't sing it without tearing up. Grace is more powerful and wonderful than most Christians know.

And for the first time in my life, all aspects of the Bible seemed to come together. Prior to learning these truths, there were parts of the Bible that seemed to contradict each other. Like when Paul writes that we're saved by grace and it's not of works—only for James to write that faith without works is dead.[41] The two seemed polar opposites, but now I know they both are true. We are saved by grace, not by works—but as believers we are called to do good works, and those works are already ordained for us by God. He will complete the works! He alone gets the glory.

Hope, Freedom, and Contentment

These truths deepen a believer's faith. They give the believer an incredible sense of freedom that cannot be explained prior to his or her understanding them. I believe I now know why Jesus proclaimed that "the truth shall make you free."[42] I certainly can't speak for everyone, but I had felt like I had to earn God's love and approval every day. Some days, I felt completely inadequate and unworthy of His love. It felt like I was walking on a tightrope, hoping not to fall off.

> The exact opposite of a "license to sin" is what happens. The Spirit inside convicts us, and He lets us know that the sin we see is not consistent with *who* we are. A "license to sin" is invalid and impossible for those who are in Christ.

It was only after learning these truths that I understood I am safe and secure in the Father's grip, and the price for my sins has once and for all been paid. That's a message of freedom, but it seems that many churches would rather have their congregations walk the tightrope. Just last night I drove by a church in my hometown that was displaying a big sign out front that read, *Yield to God and you will not yield to sin.* To me, that's a sign of bondage, not freedom. First, I'm not sure how one yields to God—and even if you know exactly how to do it, how much "yielding" would be enough? If it were my sign, it would read, *Rest in God and the rest will follow.* God wants us to be secure and to rest in Him.

Many people will say that all this talk of freedom and resting in what God will do sounds like I am advocating a "license to sin." Nothing could be further from the truth. First off, if you're a true believer, Christ is your life,[43] and that is not a life of sin. Second, when I see sin in my flesh, I am more convicted than ever before. The exact opposite of a "license to sin" is what happens. The Spirit inside convicts us, and He lets us know that the sin we see is not consistent with *who* we are. A "license to sin" is invalid and impossible for those who are in Christ. I believe this argument goes away when we fully understand the subtleties of these truths.

Where Do You Go from Here?

So, what do you do if you are like I was—you want to immediately run out and tell everyone and anyone who's willing to listen? Take it from me—exercise restraint. Walk before you run. One of the hardest parts of writing this book was resisting the temptation to get too "theological." I've only given you the tip of the iceberg of these truths. There's more to learn, and I continue to learn everyday. The Bible is the most wonderful book of all time, and I am amazed on a daily basis of the wisdom it contains.

What I'm suggesting is, if these truths ring true for you, go to the Word and study for yourself. If you're like me, you'll initially find more questions than answers. That's to be expected. It takes a while sometimes, for adults especially, to relearn things we think we already know. Make sure you are grounded in at least the basics of these truths before you share them with others.

You may ask, Is that what I did? Of course not. I began sharing these truths immediately. Undoubtedly some of you will do the same. It's natural to want to share "good news." Just be careful and be gentle. Be careful because there's no shortage of people who will delight in knocking you off your perch. If you're not careful, they will not only resist you but will leave you questioning your newfound knowledge. I urge you, as one who has trod the ground in front of you, walk before you run. You'll be more effective if you've spent sufficient time in the Word before you counsel others.

It's also a good idea to introduce these truths gently. (This is next to impossible for me.) I began this book by talking about being shocking, and I conclude by urging everyone to be gentle. What gives? Well, even shock can be gentle. When my friend Glenna Salsbury hit me over the head with these truths, she didn't just leave me bleeding in the ditch. She showed me where to look in Scripture to find what I needed. She gently guided me as I struggled to understand what I was reading.

Everyone struggles with at least some aspects of these truths at first. It requires gentle persuasion and guidance. The best way I know how to be gentle is to use Scripture. I don't want anyone to think I am editorializing, but rather that I am quoting the Word. A believer may be tempted to argue with *me,* but arguing with the Bible is not something too many Christians want to partake in.

Of course, there are differences in how people interpret what they read. Notice I didn't say there were differences in interpretation. I believe the Bible was meant for only one interpretation, and that was the truth. Truth has only one meaning. The apostle Peter underscores this point:

> *No prophecy of Scripture is of any private interpretation, for prophecy never came by the will of man, but holy men of God spoke as they were moved by the Holy Spirit* (2 Peter 1:20-21).

The differences in how we interpret the Bible stem from our position, not God's. In other words, we see different interpretations because of our individual views and circumstances.

Try to remember you don't know the perspective of the other person when you're attempting to convey these truths. All you can do is share your sincere beliefs and let God do the rest. God will reveal to all of us what He chooses to reveal—nothing more and nothing less. Christ works through our actions, and through our thoughts and beliefs. We do as we're led to do and trust that God's plan will be done. Therefore, the only way to share truths is with a gentle heart, trusting the outcome to God.

$\backsim\!\!\infty$

My great and only hope is that you will see the glory intended in these truths. I can attest only to what they've done in my walk with the Lord; I hope God chooses to do the same for everyone who reads this. The best possible outcome of this book is that you be driven to the Bible to find the answers God wants you to find. *7 Biblical Truths You Won't Hear in Church* is only the catalyst to point you to the truth. The only truth is, was, and always will be God's Word.

God is bigger, stronger, and more in control than most of us imagine. It's time to start talking about that. We need to set aside religion and find truth. Only then will we find true peace and rest. We need to nestle in His amazing grace. We once were lost, but now we're found. We were blind, but now we see. His grace is sufficient for all of us. Spread the Word.

Notes

1. This happened almost literally. See Acts 9:3-4.

2. According to a Barna Research survey from January 2000, only 38 percent of adult Americans believed that absolute truth existed. That's a shockingly low number, but it gets worse. By November 2001, that number had dropped almost by half, to 22 percent.

3. John 8:32.

4. Matthew 19:16-22 and Mark 10:17-22.

5. James 4:17.

6. Hebrews 10:17.

7. See Isaiah 64:6.

8. See John 3:3-6.

9. The "law" as referred to in the Old Testament is the entire Mosaic Law, which includes but is not limited to just the Ten Commandments.

10. See Romans 2:12, and 1 Timothy 1:9.

11. Exodus 20:1-17.

12. 2 Corinthians 12:7.

13. Romans 2:15.

14. John 11:26.

15. This is a source of much debate. The New International Version uses the terms *flesh* and *sin nature* synonomously, but they are different things. As believers, we still obviously have flesh, but our sin nature is a thing of the past. Jesus doesn't have a sin nature, and our identity is now one with Him.

16. Romans 8:1.

17. 1 Corinthians 2:16.

18. Psalm 3:8.

19. Charles Spurgeon, *Morning and Evening,* June 8 evening reading (Grand Rapids, MI: Zondervan Publishing), p. 321.

20. John Piper, *The Pleasures of God* (Sisters, OR: Multnomah, 2000), p. 243.

21. 1 Corinthians 1:31.

22. Colossians 1:16.

23. Matthew 6:8.

24. Hebrews 4:3.

25. It's important to note that, according to John 9:31, God does not hear the prayer of sinners. He only hears the prayers of His worshippers.

26. Hebrews 4:3.

27. Ephesians 1:11.

28. 2 Peter 1:3.

29. Psalms 46:1.

30. The Hebrew word *qavah* means "to expect hopefully."

31. See 2 Corinthians 12:7 for an example.

32. John 15:19.

33. Jeremiah 13:23.

34. 2 Corinthians 3:7.

35. Isaiah 64:6.

36. 1 Thessalonians 5:23-24.

37. Hebrews 10:17.

38. Philippians 4:7.

39. John 10:28-29.

40. Psalm 23:4.

41. James 2:17.

42. John 8:32.

43. Colossians 3:4.

About GraceCamp Ministries

Mission Statement

We exist to serve by helping Christians explore and discover the glory of God's grace and sovereignty, and to promote rest in Jesus Christ.

Explore. Discover. Rest!

GraceCamp Ministries is a brand-new ministry geared around three simple words: Explore. Discover. Rest! We believe that through the mostly unexplored truths of the Bible, you will discover peace, contentment, and rest that eludes most Christians. We also believe most churches do an excellent job teaching the truths surrounding "the child's grip"—how you can hold on more tightly to God. GraceCamp focuses on the truths surrounding "the Father's grip"—how the Father has a secure hold on you. (See pages 23–25 in this book.)

David Rich speaks to groups at...

- worship services
- church retreats
- special services and programs
- Christian conferences and events

As you're uplifted and encouraged, you'll see why David is one of the country's leading professional speakers. If you are part of a church or Christian organization and would like David to speak to your group, please call 1-800-717-7424 or contact us through www.GraceCamp.com.

More Resources to Help You Grow
from Harvest House Publishers

From Faking It to Finding Grace
Connie Cavanaugh

Spiritual dryness and disillusionment—nobody ever talks about them. But the truth is, almost every believer experiences periods of dry faith or feeling disconnected from God. Sadly, nearly everyone stays quiet about their doubts, and they feel alone at a time when they need support more than ever.

Connie Cavanaugh, featured columnist for *HomeLife* magazine, breaks the silence. Because she speaks out of her own ten-year struggle, you can trust her to help lead you toward a deeper and more mature friendship with God. Compassionately, she says,

- "You may feel empty and alienated, but you're not alone in this."

- "Don't try to get back to where you think you once were. Look ahead instead of back."

- "Get ready to listen to the Father, who's never stopped loving you."

- "Hold on to hope—He's calling you back."

Lifetime Guarantee
Bill Gillham

You've tried fixing your marriage, your kids, your friends, your job. Suddenly the light dawns. It's not your problems that need fixing, it's your life!

But there's good news. God doesn't ask you to live *your* life for Christ—He wants you to let His Son live *His* life through you. Jesus is the only one who has ever lived the Christian life, and He's the only one who can live it today. That's why God can offer you a lifetime guarantee of abundant living.

"I have seen...lives changed in the most beautiful way
through God's principles in Lifetime Guarantee.*"*

—Dr. Charles Stanley

Experiencing the Romance of God's Amazing Love

A Divine Invitation

Steve McVey

Have you ever wondered...*What exactly does God want from me?*

God's resounding answer is, "I want *you!*"

For years, author Steve McVey's life message has been about the riches of God's grace. And yet he admits, "I feel like Lucy Ricardo on the production line at the candy factory. I can't keep up and I can't swallow anymore...I allowed the mechanics of ministry and 'living a Christian life' to rob me of the exhilarating awareness of the indwelling presence of Christ."

From that awareness, Steve was awakened to an invitation from God...a divine invitation to the kind of intimacy God wants you and every child of His to enjoy.

Grace Amazing

Steve McVey

If your Christian life seems as dry as dust and you're just going around in circles...*maybe you're wandering in the wilderness.*

In the wilderness, you feel as though...

- you live by the rules, and the Bible is the rule book

- you work hard for God...but you never quite measure up

In the land of God's amazing grace, you experience the truth that...

- God has made you alive *in Christ*—and now you want to do what He wants

- Jesus has done all the work, and you can rest in the Father's acceptance

Steve McVey reveals to you more of the heart of your loving, giving Father...so you can better grasp just why His grace is so amazing.

"I strongly urge you to get Becoming Who God Intended *and put it to work in your life."*

—Josh McDowell

Becoming Who God Intended

David Eckman

Whether you realize it or not, your imagination is filled with *pictures* of reality. The Bible indicates these pictures reveal your true "heart beliefs"—the beliefs that actually shape your everyday feelings and reactions to family, friends, and others, to life's circumstances, and to God.

Perhaps you're

- struggling with anxiety, guilt, or habitual sins

- frustrated because your experience doesn't seem to match what the Bible talks about

- wondering if your emotions and feelings fit into the Christian life at all

David Eckman compassionately shows you how to allow God's Spirit to build new, *biblical* pictures in your heart and imagination. As you do this, you will be able to accept God's acceptance of you in Christ, break free of negative emotions and habitual sins...and finally experience the life God the Father has always intended for you.

"David Eckman is a man you can trust...
His teaching resonates with God's wisdom and compassion."

—**Stu Weber,** author of *Tender Warrior*
and *Four Pillars of a Man's Heart*